Wiley Trading Advantage

Beyond Candlesticks / Steve Nison
Beyond Technical Analysis / Tushar Chande
Campaign Trading / John Sweeney
Contrary Opinion / R. Earl Hadady
Cybernetic Trading Strategies / Murray A. Ruggiero Jr.
Day Trade Part-Time / John Cook and Jeanette Szwec
Encyclopedia of Chart Patterns / Thomas Bulkowski
Expert Trading Systems / John R. Wolberg
Fundamental Analysis / Jack Schwager
Gaming the Market / Ronald B. Shelton
Genetic Algorithms and Investment Strategies / Richard J. Bauer Jr.
Intermarket Technical Analysis / John J. Murphy
Long-Term Secrets to Short-Term Trading / Larry Williams
Macro Trading and Investment Strategies / Gabriel Burstein
Managed Trading / Jack Schwager
McMillan on Options / Lawrence G. McMillan
Neural Network Time Series Forecasting of Financial Markets / E. Michael Azoff
New Market Timing Techniques / Thomas R. DeMark
New Trading Dimensions / Bill Williams
Nonlinear Pricing / Christopher T. May
Option Market Making / Alan J. Baird
Option Strategies, Second Edition / Courtney Smith
Pattern, Price & Time/ James A. Hyerczyk
Point and Figure Charting / Thomas J. Dorsey
Profits from Natural Resources / Roland A. Jansen
Schwager on Futures/ Jack Schwager
Seasonality / Jake Bernstein
Stock Index Futures & Options / Susan Abbott Gidel
Study Guide for Trading for a Living / Dr. Alexander Elder
Study Guide to Accompany Fundamental Analysis / Jack Schwager
Study Guide to Accompany Technical Analysis/ Jack Schwager
Technical Analysis / Jack Schwager
Technical Analysis of the Options Markets / Richard Hexton
Technical Market Indicators / Richard J. Bauer Jr., and Julie R. Dahlquist
The Day Trader's Manual / William F. Eng
The Dynamic Option Selection System / Howard L. Simons
The Hedge Fund Edge / Mark Boucher
The Intuitive Trader / Robert Koppel
The Mathematics of Money Management / Ralph Vince
The New Market Wizards / Jack Schwager
The New Money Management / Ralph Vince
The New Options Market, Fourth Edition / Max Ansbacher
The New Science of Technical Analysis / Thomas R. DeMark
The New Technical Trader / Tushar Chande and Stanley S. Kroll
The Option Advisor / Bernie G. Schaeffer
The Options Course/ George A. Fontanills
The Options Course Workbook / George A. Fontanills
The Trader's Tax Survival Guide, Revised Edition / Ted Tesser
The Trader's Tax Solution / Ted Tesser
The Trading Game/ Ryan Jones
The Ultimate Trading Guide / John Hill, George Pruitt, and Lundy Hill
The Visual Investor / John J. Murphy
Trader Vic II / Victor Sperandeo
Trading Applications of Japanese Candlestick Charting / Gary Wagner and Brad Matheny
Trading Chaos / Bill Williams
Trading for a Living / Dr. Alexander Elder
Trading on Expectations/ Brendan Moynihan
Trading Systems & Methods, Third Edition / Perry Kaufman
Trading the Plan / Robert Deel
Trading to Win / Ari Kiev, M.D.
Trading with Crowd Psychology / Carl Gyllenram
Trading without Fear / Richard W. Arms Jr.

VALUE INVESTING IN COMMODITY FUTURES

How to Profit with Scale Trading

HAL MASOVER

JOHN WILEY & SONS, INC.
New York • Chichester • Weinheim • Brisbane • Singapore • Toronto

Published by John Wiley & Sons, Inc.
Published simultaneously in Canada.

This publication is designed to provide accurate and authoritative information in
regard to the subject matter covered. It is sold with the understanding that the
publisher is not engaged in rendering professional services. If professional advice
or other expert assistance is required, the services of a competent professional
person should be sought.

Designations used by companies to distinguish their products are often claimed as
trademarks. In all instances where John Wiley & Sons, Inc. is aware of a claim,
the product names appear in initial capital or all capital letters. Readers, however,
should contact the appropriate companies for more complete information regarding
trademarks and registration.

Library of Congress Cataloging-in-Publication Data

Masover, Hal.
    Value investing in commodity futures : how to profit with scale trading /
Hal Masover.
       p.   cm. — (Wiley trading advantage)
    ISBN 0-471-34881-3 (cloth : alk. paper)
    1. Commodity futures. 2. Futures. I. Title. II. Series.

    HG6046.M337   2001
    332.63′28—dc21   00-043739

Printed in the United States of America.

10 9 8 7 6 5 4 3 2 1

FOREWORD

Congratulations! You are about to embark on an exciting journey of opportunity aboard the ship we proudly call *Scale Trader*. We all share the desire to realize the full potential of our lives. Unfortunately, this desire goes unfulfilled in most people. Fear of failure is a more powerful motivator for many than is opportunity for success. The very fact that you have picked up a book on the emotionally charged topic of commodity investing indicates that your personal life equation is courageous; that is, you have the courage to leave no stone unturned in the search for opportunity. It is for this quality of courage that I congratulate you. After reading this book, you may decide that this particular journey does not serve your goals. If so, this will have been a successful exercise in getting you one step closer to the opportunity you seek.

By the time Hal and I came across the methodology of scale trading, we had both been in the broker role for four years. It does not take long in the hot seat to verify what we all have heard: Most commodity traders lose money. On the surface, this fact may lead you to put this book down right now. For Hal and me, it is the compelling reason to explore further. The key word here is *most*. In fact, *some* of the players in this zero-sum game *do* succeed. If you are anything at all like me, that fact is all you need to know to step aboard and make a thorough investigation of the integrity of *Scale Trader* and determine for yourself if it will carry you to the personal and financial goals you have charted.

For me, the beauty of scale trading is that it is not a system but a methodology. For many this is bad news, as the quest is for that Holy Grail black box that magically spits out profits without any input or emotional involvement from them. Yes, when I fall into a lethargic attitude about life, I also wish for such a system. If you really think about it, though, you may not really want a life where it is that easy.

Many are the examples of individuals who "have it all" (inheritance, title, etc.) but live chaotic lives, desperately seeking some confirmation that their actions make a difference. Scale trading puts you in the role of captain of the ship, where the quality of your strategic planning directly determines the success of your voyage. Without question this takes courage and discipline. However, the difference it makes between you and the average commodity trader is dramatic. Unlike the common "trader," you are never lost out at sea because *Scale Trader* provides you with a strong fundamental framework from which to chart your journey.

The principles on which this ship is built are the most sound ones that I have come across. Indeed, they are timeless and immutable. Whenever the sea gets rough, you can revisit the plan, making sure the rigging is sound and secure. If necessary, you can alter course a bit if new information requires, but stay the course confident that the principles on which you launched the voyage are the anchors that will hold you through most any storm.

Scale Trader does not pull through without testing you, however. These storms will tempt you to believe that this time the principles are not working and are not going to work. When this happens, reread this Foreword and these words: *The Principles Work!* The journey may take longer than expected, and you may have to make an appraisal as to whether you have enough food and water to get you to your goal. At these times, you as the captain may have to ration supplies, eating one meal per day instead of three, for example. But as sure as night follows day, the storm will break.

The rewards of such experiences are high. Not only are your potential profits compelling, but you get the taste of being the master of your destiny. In my opinion, this taste is the real reward of a successful voyage aboard *Scale Trader*. After all, once you truly know yourself to be the master of your destiny, then no storms within your personal life are too great to weather. Just as a seasoned sea captain, successful scale traders grow in both courage and humility. They have learned tremendous respect for the elements and yet are able to move gracefully through them, continually striking a balance between the risk of their actions and their potential reward. Working with clients to achieve this balance is the driving force behind our day-to-day life at Crown Futures. What began as an exercise to "make money" has revealed itself to be far more comprehensive and compelling.

Somewhere along the way I came across this elegantly simple equation for success:

$$\text{Preparedness} + \text{Opportunity} = \text{Success}$$

The marketplace beckons us with opportunities every moment of every day, while *Scale Trader* gives us the framework and the methodology that prepare us for the journey. It is my hope that, within this grand adventure we call life, what follows will give you the tools and the confidence necessary to create your own successful expedition.

STUART T. VALENTINE
October, 2000

ACKNOWLEDGMENTS

"If I have come a long way, it is because I have stood on the shoulders of giants." I may not have that quote exactly right. I don't remember who said it. Maybe Einstein? I'm sure some good reader will inform me of the correct quote and who said it. I am just reaching for the sentiment here. I certainly am no Einstein, but I believe I have stood on the shoulders of giants.

The biggest giant may be Robert Weist, who wrote a book on the scale trading method back in the 1970s. I bought that book in 1991 on a whim. I read it and found it made a great deal of sense. Over the years Bob has been very generous with his time, spirit, and knowledge, and I am very grateful.

Another giant worth mentioning is Peter Orange. Peter used to live here in Fairfield, Iowa, until he had a severe car accident, after which he moved to the Seattle area to be close to a world class rehab clinic. One of Peter's clients wrote a book on scale trading in which he tried to improve on scale trading by selling short the same commodity you are buying, using a different contract month if the price falls below the lowest price of your scale. This is very difficult, and an idea that is not recommended. It happened that Peter was this author's broker. One day Peter suggested that the author look at selling call options instead of futures contracts. This is an interesting idea that is discussed in this book. Thanks to Peter for his time in answering questions about how he handles this innovation.

I've also had an enormous amount of help from Bob Steele. Bob has traded grains professionally since the 1960s. Over the years he has consistently been generous with his time and ideas about trading grains. I don't know anyone with as much understanding of the fundamentals in the grain markets as Bob has, nor do I know anyone more generous with their time and knowledge.

I cannot forget to mention the many others who have helped to produce this book. Jennifer Miller was the operations officer at Crown Futures Corporation during the production of the first edition and spent many hours proofreading both grammar and content as well as performing many other chores too numerous to mention. My wife, Joan Masover, apart from being a wonderful wife and mother to our children, has been very helpful with her suggestions and proofreading.

I certainly cannot forget Mark Etzkorn. Mark wrote Appendix I, "Getting a Handle on Commodity Futures." He went over every word of text in the first edition and made innumerable suggestions on how I might express my ideas better, many of which have been incorporated in this edition. Finally, to anyone who, through their work or encouragement, made this book possible, thank you.

H.M.

CONTENTS

——

Introduction xv

PART I
AN INTRODUCTION TO A BETTER METHOD OF TRADING

Chapter 1
Scale Trading: Elegance in Trading 3

Chapter 2
How to Know When to Start Scale Trading 11

Chapter 3
Why Is Scale Trading Better Than Other Types of Trading? 25

PART II
LEARNING THE FUNDAMENTALS

Chapter 4
Fundamentals the Right Way 41

Chapter 5
Grain Market Fundamentals 49

Chapter 6
Livestock Market Fundamentals 59

Chapter 7
Metals Market Fundamentals 69

Chapter 8
Energy Market Fundamentals 81

Chapter 9
Softs Market Fundamentals 85

Chapter 10
Using Seasonal Information the Right Way 91

PART III
SCALE TRADING IN ACTION

Chapter 11
How to Construct a Scale 99

Chapter 12
Taking Profits 117

Chapter 13
The Dreaded Contract Rollovers 123

Chapter 14
Options 131

Chapter 15
Don't Skip This Chapter: Choosing a Broker 145

Appendix I
Getting a Handle on Commodity Futures: A Primer
for Beginning Traders 161

Appendix II
Other Possibly Profitable Methods   167

Appendix III
How to Construct a Scale on Your Computer   181

Glossary   185

Index   195

INTRODUCTION

Commodity traders are a wonderfully unique breed. You have to be an optimist to take the great risks involved in commodity trading. Sometimes commodity traders are more optimistic than warranted. Specifically, I am referring to the new trader with a small amount of capital. I have patiently explained to this kind of trader that their chances were not much different from winning the lottery and that they might be better off giving their money to charity. Rookie traders with insufficient capital will probably end up losing their money. The people who get that money are likely to be professional traders. The losers will likely feel bad about themselves. If they gave their money to charity instead, they could feel great about themselves, and the money would probably mean a great deal to the recipients.

This suggestion, to my knowledge, has never been followed by those to whom I have spoken. The most common response is one of almost impossible optimism. "I'm not average. The average investor isn't very bright," they say. "I'm one of the ten percent that will make money." I know I feel that way. If you're like me, an eternal optimist, you're going to need some help. Optimism must be combined with a logical, effective trading approach that helps keep the odds on your side.

The method described in this book is precisely such a strategy. It is the best help I know for traders who want a common-sense approach to the commodity futures markets. Whether you are a newcomer to commodities or an old salt, scale trading can offer you a new perspective on commodity trading and help improve your long-term performance.

Commodity trading is enticing, but finding clear and reliable information on it can be difficult. As a result, too many traders enter the markets without really understanding what they are getting into. Maybe you read a book on commodities that made it all seem so easy and so certain. Maybe you traded on paper for a while and watched profits mount up until you couldn't stand it anymore; you just had to get some of that. So you opened an account with a little money. (I know—the $5,000 minimum of most brokerages doesn't seem like a "little" money!) Sometime between three weeks and six months later, with $1,200 left in your account, it suddenly dawned on you, "This isn't as easy as I thought."

So you went back to the drawing board, bought some more books, subscribed to a newsletter or two, and maybe even bought a commercially available system. You put some more money in your account, and, after all that work, you got the same result—more money down the drain and your goal no closer than when you started. I truly hope this story is not starting to sound familiar to you, but I've been involved in commodities since 1987, and I've witnessed this type of scenario hundreds, maybe thousands, of times.

AN APPRENTICESHIP IN THE COMMODITY MARKETS

My own story is illustrative. After investing in real estate successfully in the early 1980s, I began investing in stocks in 1986. That year I ended my real estate career by moving from Philadelphia, a city of 1.5 million people, to Fairfield, Iowa, a small town of only 10,000 people. I've never believed in small-town real estate, so I started looking for another career.

A commodity brokerage firm hired me, and I got my license. But before actually working for that firm, I quit, realizing I wouldn't be happy there. In the process I'd become fascinated with commodities. I opened an account and made my first trade in January 1987. I bought a Standard & Poor's (S&P) futures contract. In two days I made $2,500. "This is for me!" I thought.

With the S&P making new record highs, I thought, "This can't go on forever." I reversed my position short, and in two days I lost $5,000. Ouch!

In shock, I closed out the position and thought, "I better study a little more and figure out what I'm doing." I hit the books and started looking into computer-based trading. After doing a little research, I bought a software program for $1,000. This program seemed to be based on sound logic, at least to my novice brain, and was designed to give clear entries and exits. All I had to do was feed the program daily price data, and it would spit out what I was to do. I don't remember how much I lost before I put that program away forever. I wrote it off as tuition payments to the great trading school of hard knocks and continued studying.

I spent another $250 on another computer program (once wasn't enough), and this time I got lucky. I found a broker who had the program, and he placed the orders for me while I went traveling. During the summer I made $2,500 with this program, but by fall the magic was failing. After losing $1,500 of my profits, I did the first truly smart thing of my brief trading career. I stopped trading it. I kept following the results of this program for a couple of years. It never made money again.

Still looking for help, I turned to newsletters and hotlines, the "gurus" of commodities. For the most part, this was an abysmal failure. Unfortunately, the one bright exception (who made me so much money that I finished $8,000 ahead in 1987) stopped publishing his hotline, and I was left searching for the holy grail again.

Most investors would be tickled to make $8,000 on a $25,000 trading account, but I had been doing this full time. I needed an income. I also realized that I didn't know what I was doing. All my profits were from a guru who was out of business and a computer program that didn't work anymore.

After spending all year trading commodities, I decided the best thing to do was to use my license and become a broker. This would give me the ability to stay close to the markets that fascinated me and to use other people's money to learn about trading. I truly feel sorry for those kind souls who trusted me and thought I knew what I was doing. For the next several years any customers who followed my advice lost money.

THE PAYOFF

I finally turned the corner when I found an approach called *scale trading*. It made perfect sense to me. It seemed to be a way to take advantage of the natural behavior of commodities markets. Once I started to use it for my clients, everything changed. From the first customer whom I was able to persuade to trade based on this method,

I found a different world. This was the first time I had something that I could actually offer to people without fear that they would most likely lose all their money. Until then, roughly from 1987 to 1991, I lost more money than any one person could afford to lose, unless they were extremely wealthy, and then it wouldn't have been fun.

The point is, most investors can't afford to make the mistakes that I have made in order to learn from them. They will go broke long before they develop wisdom. I sincerely hope that you will be able to profit from understanding and avoiding my mistakes. Reviewing my story, I can point out several common mistakes. If you've made them yourself, they'll be easy to spot. If not, don't worry; we'll be going over them and others in the course of the book.

It is important to point out that I did not invent the method that will be discussed here. This method has been around for quite awhile. In the mid-1970s Bob Weist published a four-page pamphlet about a method called "Scale Trading." Scale trading described in this book is the very same method. It has served my clients well over the years. We are extremely grateful to Bob Weist for developing this method and sharing it with us.

We have worked with scale trading since 1992 and have come to believe that investors need a couple of tools in addition to pure scale trading. These tools are described in Part II, in which I detail how to do your own fundamental analysis and how to apply that analysis to your scale trading (Chapter 10, "Using Seasonal Information the Right Way," and Chapter 14, "Options," respectively).

It is important to understand the risks of commodity trading. Commodity trading involves an extreme amount of leverage. That leverage allows for tremendous gains but also for tremendous losses. Various risk-control methods may not work in all circumstances. Also, remember that although this book discusses methods that may have worked in the past, past performance is no guarantee of future results.

VALUE INVESTING IN COMMODITY FUTURES

PART I

AN INTRODUCTION TO A BETTER METHOD OF TRADING

Part I introduces you to scale trading and shows you why it is a better approach to trading than other methodologies.

1

SCALE TRADING:
ELEGANCE IN TRADING

Scale trading is one of the simplest, easiest, and most elegant methods of trading I have ever seen. I have searched for years trying to come up with something better. Although I have found a few good things and a lot of promising ideas, I have still not found anything that has proved better. Scale trading offers a way for individuals, even those with relatively modest amounts of capital, to use some of the same methods the big boys use.

Have you ever imagined what it would be like to be one of the big boys? Can you see yourself wading into the trading pit, with everyone's eyes on you to see what you're going to do? Or do you see yourself trading from a large, richly appointed office atop some urban skyscraper? Did you ever see the movie *Trading Places* with Eddie Murphy? Murphy plays a street beggar who magically winds up living our fantasy of trading big time in the pits and in a fancy downtown office. And, son of a gun, he's good at it (only in the movies)!

I mention this fantasy because I have seen one trader after another seduced by it. Commodity trading can be an exhilarating and highly profitable experience, but it can also bring financial ruin on the unprepared or foolhardy. Although most people are aware of the possibility of ruin, they don't really believe it can happen to them. Because they don't really believe that, they never make plans to avoid it. Instead, they try to pull off some sort of real-life *Trading Places,* taking huge risks in the hope (always a bad word in trading) of reaping a huge profit. Often they find that instead of leaping into the big time, they fall into deep losses.

3

The reality of trading is usually quite different from the fantasies. I'm not aware of any big traders who really trade like the individuals in our fantasy. Although they do have a wide variety of styles, from long-term systematic commodity fund managers (whose trades last months or even years) to short-term pit traders (who never hold positions for more than 30 seconds), the successful ones I have come to know are very sober. No matter what kind of approach they use, they are realistic about their chances in the commodity markets, and they have a definite plan to make money.

TAKING A CUE FROM THE BIG TRADERS

We want to discuss one very sane and sober way that many large traders trade. This method was first developed as an adaptation of gambling methods used in Las Vegas. It can be used for gambling, stocks, and commodities. Although the method can work in all three areas as well as other areas of investment, it is particularly effective in commodity futures for a number of reasons that we will discuss shortly.

But first, to help you understand the method, let's fantasize a little more. Imagine that you work for a company with a huge fleet of cars and delivery trucks. Perhaps it's one of the delivery companies, like FedEx or UPS. Your job is to help the company control fuel costs. A critical part of your job involves buying futures contracts of unleaded gas to protect the company against a rise in prices (the process called *hedging* that we discuss in Appendix I, "Getting a Handle on Commodity Futures"). If you only needed to buy one contract, your job would be simple. You call a broker and buy at a time when you believe prices are cheap to lock in a low price for your company. This is a very large company, and one contract equals only 42,000 gallons. I have no idea how long it would take a nationwide fleet of trucks to use 42,000 gallons, but I wouldn't be surprised if it were less than an hour.

To implement your program adequately, you might need to buy thousands of contracts. As I write this, the most active contract for unleaded gas is the February 2000 contract. There are approximately 16,000 contracts of open interest (the number of contracts being held overnight). On January 26, 2000, approximately 16,500 contracts traded during the trading session (Figure 1.1). If you were to go into

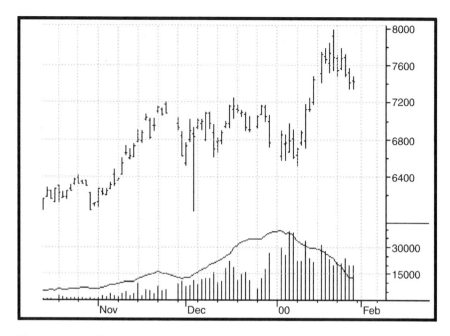

Figure 1.1 February 2000 unleaded gasoline futures. (*Source:* OmegaResearch)

this market and attempt to buy, say, 2,000 contracts all at once, you might shock the market because your one order would represent almost 12.5 percent of the contracts traded all day. Because you probably wouldn't find one individual seller who would want to sell you that much, you'd have to keep bidding up the price to coax more traders to sell. In the end you would have created your own minirally in which your company would be chasing its own tail, paying ever higher prices for its gasoline contracts. At least in the short term, you would not have protected your company from higher prices. You actually would have created an artificially high price for your company to pay.

SCALING IN AND OUT

The way you might solve this problem is to do exactly what many large traders usually do: scale in your purchases. Once you have determined the approximate price at which you would like to buy, you would begin to buy at (you hope) progressively lower prices within a target range. When you buy small allotments at a time, it is usually much easier to find a seller for each buy order. You thereby may avoid the possibility of scaring the market higher. Scaling in your purchases also has the advantage of helping you buy at progressively lower prices if the market continues to decline after your initial purchases.

You might also implement the same program in reverse when it comes time to liquidate your position, and for the same reasons—if you sell all your contracts at once, you can have a temporarily depressing effect on the market, and you might find yourself getting filled at progressively lower prices. By selling on a scale-up basis, you might even—and hopefully will—sell at progressively higher prices should the market continue to rise after you make your initial sell.

Before we leave this particular fantasy, it's important to realize that a large commercial firm is in a very good position to know when to buy and when to sell. After all, our imaginary delivery company is in the market to buy unleaded gas every day, all day long.

Because buying gas is an important part of the company's costs, part of controlling that cost means getting a handle on when prices are likely to rise and to fall. Such firms usually have full-time analysts whose job is to gather as much information as possible and to make projections of what prices are likely to do. Although they may not always get their projections of price movement right, their intimate knowledge of the market gives them the chance to get it right most of the time.

In our fantasy about being a large trader, I have presented two important elements of the method of trading we wish to discuss: (1) scaling in and out and (2) knowledge of a market's tendencies. Our fantasy was that of being a commercial trader, but we could have presented the same principles with only slight and, for our purposes, insignificant differences were we to fantasize about any other type of large trader. Regardless of your trading goal, it can be more practical to scale in and out of large trades than to try to go in and out in a block. A thorough understanding of the market you are trading is a prerequisite for any trader—you have to know how the market behaves to apply this or any other approach successfully.

The genius of the scale trading method is that it gives small individual traders the ability to emulate a trading method that the big boys use. Although the system was developed as an adaptation of a gambling system, it accidentally resulted in giving the individual a very simple, yet very sophisticated, tool used by megatraders. It is a simple but powerful approach that does not require familiarity with advanced mathematical calculations or complex indicators—just knowledge of how a market behaves.

Scale trading, as it is called, involves buying a commodity at progressively lower prices until it stops declining. You then sell the commodity at progressively higher prices as it rises. An illustration will help you see how this works: Suppose you believe that corn prices are approaching a bottom. Using the scale trading method, you might begin to buy corn at specific intervals, maybe every five cents down. You might buy a contract at $2.45, $2.40, $2.35, $2.30, and so forth. If corn prices stopped going down at $2.27, you would own four contracts. Suppose you decide that you would be content to make $400 profit per contract. Every penny in corn is worth $50. To make $400 per contract, you would have to sell each contract at an 8-cent profit. If the price rises after bottoming at $2.27, you would need to sell at $2.38, $2.43, $2.48, and $2.53 to achieve your 8-cent profit per contract. This, in its simplest form, is how to scale in and scale out.

ADVANTAGES TO SCALE TRADING

With this method, the small trader borrows one of the big traders' methods for entering and exiting positions. There are two advantages to trading this way that immediately come to mind. First, the method buys weakness and sells strength. Second, the trader doesn't have to be perfect.

Buy Low and Sell High

By buying at progressively lower prices and selling at progressively higher prices, you set up an automatic mechanism for buying low and selling high—precisely what all traders want to do.

Time and time again I have found that scale traders are taking their profits when everyone else is getting excited about a market. Maybe the news media has just reported that it hasn't rained in Iowa for six weeks and the temperature is hitting 100 degrees. The corn market will usually run up on this news. The scale trader who may have bought when nobody else was much interested in corn will be able to sell into this rally when everyone else is buying.

Many times I have seen that, just when the scale trader is regretting having sold all their contracts because the market looks as if it's going to scream higher, something happens, such as rain in Iowa or a temperature drop into the 70s. The price of corn plummets, creating losses and misery for those who were buying higher during the rally and allowing the scale trader, once again, to buy low after having sold his or her contracts to those poor souls who bought high.

There are some occasions when, for good reason, scale traders regret selling all their contracts on a rally. The market really does run up in a sustained rally that is very profitable for people who follow trends and not for scale traders. This may be perceived by some as a weakness in the scale trading method. It is important to realize that these types of rallies occur infrequently and that trying to trade in a way that will capitalize on them is what often leads to the ruin of traders. However, later in the book I will discuss an adaptation of scale trading that may allow the scale trader to participate in these infrequent monster rallies without significant risk.

You Don't Have to Be Perfect

It is very fortunate that scale traders don't have to be perfect because most people, including me, are not perfect. What I mean is that in scale trading we build a position. If you trade using some of the popular methods, such as buying 1-2-3 bottoms or selling head-and-shoulders tops, you will probably put all your contracts on at once.

If you have a small account, your position may be only one contract. Doing things this way, it's important to have a plan that, among other things, deals with what to do when you are wrong. This usually involves using a stop order. Suppose you buy corn at $2.45 and decide to risk maybe $500 on the trade. Then when corn drops to $2.27, as in the preceding example, you will have been stopped out at $2.35 with a $500 loss. When the market later rallies to $2.53 and higher, you probably won't be in it because you were stopped out with a loss earlier.

Trading in this more traditional and more popular way means you have to be almost perfect. If you're going to try to buy a bottom, the market better rally now or you're going to lose money. In scale trading, by contrast, you "build" a position gradually, so you don't need to be so precise. Because you are buying at progressively lower prices, you don't need to have the market turn on a dime; you can give it a pretty wide range and still come out very well. Not being perfect myself, I like any system that is this forgiving.

A couple of questions naturally arise. First, how do you know when to begin a program of scale-down buying? Second, how much capital does this take? We'll cover the question of capital later in the book. Right now, let's proceed to discuss how to know when to start your scale.

2

HOW TO KNOW WHEN TO START SCALE TRADING

THE FLEXING OF SUPPLY AND DEMAND

I mentioned in Chapter 1 that the scale trading method may apply to other forms of investment but works best with commodities. The principle reason for this is economics. The most basic law of economics taught to everyone who takes Economics 101 in college is the law of supply and demand. This law is very simple (Figure 2.1): If supply shrinks and demand remains constant, prices will rise, on the other hand, if supply expands while demand remains constant, prices drop. If supply remains constant while demand increases, prices rise; if supply remains constant while demand decreases, prices decline.

In the real world, supply and demand are usually both in flux. One of the main reasons for fluctuations in demand is the principle of elasticity. If the price of something rises too high, it tends to choke off demand. Therefore, demand is described as having a certain elasticity. Some commodities are more elastic than others, but virtually all commodities have some degree of demand elasticity. For example, the demand for gold jewelry is quite elastic, whereas the demand for electricity is relatively inelastic. (You need power more than you need a new gold pendant.)

Elasticity also applies to supply. If prices rise enough, producers of that commodity rush to produce more to maximize profits at higher prices. Some commodities are more supply elastic than others, but all have some degree of elasticity.

11

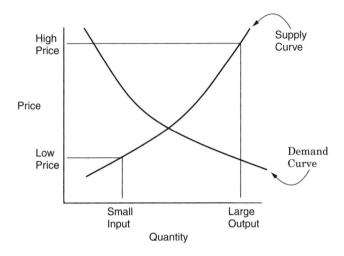

Figure 2.1   Supply and demand curve.

Elasticity contributes to the boom-bust cycle of commodities. Take a look at the 20-year soybean chart (Figure 2.2). For the past 20 years, every time the price of soybeans rose to $9 per bushel or higher it was a short-lived affair. Why? Because every soybean farmer planted every square foot of land he could in soybeans, thus increasing supply and causing the price to drop.

Notice also that prices below $5.50, while less volatile, also tended to be short-lived. Farmers are less interested in planting soybeans at those prices and will look to shift acreage to corn in the Midwest or cotton in the South.

Demand is also working to create these price swings. At $5 buyers around the world are eager to stockpile all the soybeans farmers want to sell. But at $10 they tend to buy only what they absolutely need.

This economic cycle of commodity supply and demand explains why we choose to use scale trading for commodities rather than some other investment vehicle. The interaction of supply and demand creates practical low ranges for commodity prices that provide scale traders with practical levels to build scale positions. When the price of a commodity approaches levels where it has bottomed historically and then reverses to the upside, scale traders have an opportunity to build their position. Figures 2.3 to 2.6 show long-term charts for corn, wheat, pork bellies, and crude oil, respectively, so that you may

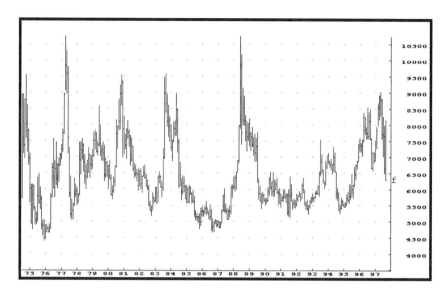

Figure 2.2   Monthly soybean chart. (*Source:* FutureSource/Bridge)

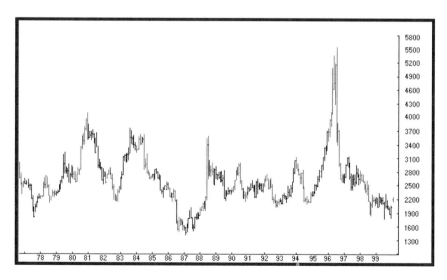

Figure 2.3   Monthly corn chart. (*Source:* FutureSource/Bridge)

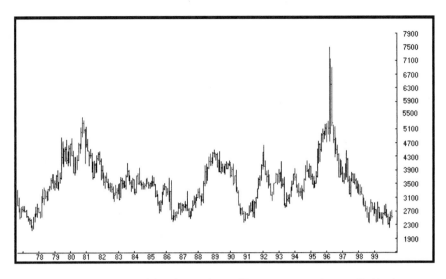

Figure 2.4   Monthly wheat chart. (*Source:* FutureSource/Bridge)

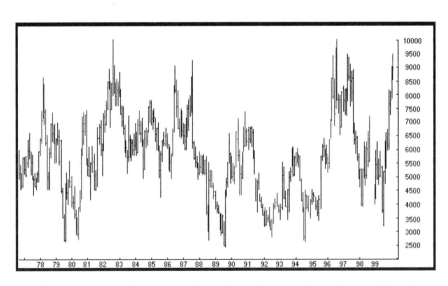

Figure 2.5   Monthly pork bellies chart. (*Source:* FutureSource/Bridge)

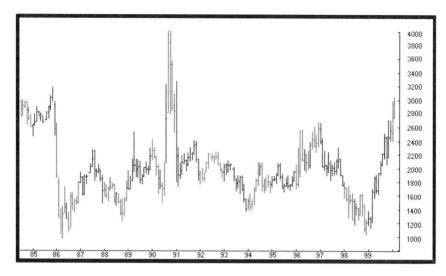

Figure 2.6 Monthly crude oil chart. (*Source:* FutureSource/Bridge)

see the cyclical nature of commodity prices. You can see that it is because of this cyclical nature, dictated by the interaction of supply and demand, that a method such as scale trading is well suited to take advantage of such fluctuating conditions.

There is always demand for soybeans. In fact, as the world's population increases and the third world develops, that demand increases steadily year after year and is especially large when soybeans are cheap. It is hard to imagine that soybeans or corn or wheat or cattle or silver or any other physical commodity could ever become valueless—a commodity's price will not go to zero. Therefore, we know that when we begin to buy a commodity on a scale-down basis, there is always a floor.

A stock, on the other hand, most certainly can become valueless and often does. The 12 companies in the original 1897 Dow Jones Industrial Average were the blue chips, the best and the biggest. But, after a hundred years, most of them are long gone. But a hundred years ago wheat futures were being traded at the Chicago Board of Trade, and they will still be trading a hundred years from now, even if there is no more Chicago Board of Trade.

A commodity cannot go out of business, but a company can. And any of that company's stock that you bought on a scale-down basis will become worthless. If I'm going to engage in buying something at progressively lower prices, I feel a lot safer knowing that the bottom price is likely to be well above zero.

Furthermore, if a company were poorly managed, it might not go out of business, but its value as a company might never go up. The stocks of many companies have not participated in the roaring bull market of the past 13 years. The value of a commodity, on the other hand, does not decline because of poor business management. Its price declines because of changes in supply and demand.

There is a wonderful old saying in commodities, "Nothing cures low prices like low prices." When prices drop, demand tends to increase. This often occurs at the same time that production may begin to contract because it is unprofitable. The greater demand and smaller supply brought about by production cutbacks will reduce any surplus supply, and prices inevitably will rise.

Are there any exceptions to this law? None that I can think of. It is true that there are many commodities that were much higher priced at one time than they are today. We once had 66-cent sugar and $850 gold. But the law does not say that the price will return to extremely high prices because there were some unusual circumstances in the past. It only says that a low price will stimulate demand and discourage production, thus eventually leading to a tightness of supply that will result in higher prices. Some commodities have gone to extreme low prices, but eventually the law catches up with them and prices rise again.

Clearly, deciding on the price at which you will begin your program of buying is very important. It can make the difference between the success and the failure of your program. Before we discuss this subject in detail, we will first turn to another critical consideration in scale trading: Which futures markets should you use for this method?

WHAT IS A COMMODITY?

The law of supply and demand applies to commodities. In recent years, however, a new kind of market has arisen—financial futures. Financial futures include stock indexes (such as the Standard & Poor's 500), interest rates (such as U.S. Treasury bond futures), and currency futures (such as the U.S. Dollar Index and Japanese yen). Financial futures are not commodities. I know that supply and demand do have an influence on financial futures, but supply and demand are usually not the driving force behind the prices of these instruments. Avoid them, at least for scale trading, unless you have practically unlimited capital.

The principles of scale trading do eventually apply to these markets. The problem is that the very large size of the contracts combined with the huge range of possible prices means that scale trading these futures would require far more capital than is commonly available to an individual. I honestly don't know how much capital is necessary, but I can tell you that I would feel that $100,000 was way too little. In fact, I would be quite frightened to try to scale trade a financial future with only $100,000.

Consider a comparison between a wheat contract and a Standard & Poor's (S&P) 500 Index contract. In early 2000 the price of wheat was about $2.60 per bushel. With 5,000 bushels in a contract of wheat, the total value of a wheat contract then was about $13,000. In early 2000 the S&P 500 was trading around 1400. The contract multiplier is $250, so the value of a contract was $350,000. It *is* doable to create a scale for the S&P. When we cover how to construct a scale in Chapter 11, you might try constructing one for the S&P. Simple arithmetic will tell you a lot, however. The S&P contract was almost 27 times larger than a wheat contract in early 2000.

Then there is the nature of these markets to consider. Commodities are cyclical due to the large influence of supply and demand, but financial futures display no such regular cycles. Consider what it might have been like to scale Treasury bonds during the severe decline in the value of these instruments in the late 1970s and early 1980s when the prime rate exceeded 20 percent. Would you have felt that $100,000 was enough to scale trade stock indexes during the 1987 stock market crash? What about the decline of the yen during the late 1990s? These markets are just so huge and are subject to so many considerations other than supply and demand that scale trading them may well be a fast way to financial ruin.

Financial futures, for our purposes, have no intrinsic value. What I mean to say is that they are paper assets that, in and of themselves, are valueless except for the value we assign them. I am not using double-talk here. What is the value of a one dollar bill? It has an infinitesimal value as paper and ink. Any other value is an arbitrary value we bestow on it as a medium of exchange. Its *intrinsic value* is simply its value as paper and ink. All financial futures are futures on financial instruments that share these value characteristics.

This is quite different from the value of nonfinancial futures. These commodities have utility in and of themselves. Their prices may fluctuate considerably, but they continue to have intrinsic value. What I mean is that we can use them for something. This intrinsic value will usually constitute most, if not all, of the price they command at any given time. For this reason their price fluctuations do not have the seemingly limitless quality that financial futures have. Hard commodities rarely stray far from their intrinsic value, whereas financial futures bear no relationship to their intrinsic value. This is why we stick to hard commodities. It is far easier to figure out their value at any given time.

RULE NUMBER ONE: SCALE ONLY FROM THE LONG SIDE

Along with deciding between financial and commodity futures, we need to consider whether to employ both long and short scales or just one or the other. As stated earlier, we choose to restrict ourselves to the long side only. We never scale from the short side. We use sell orders only for taking profits. This is a very important point, and the reason for it is simple: A commodity cannot go to zero or lower. On the other hand, we cannot determine what its upper limit might be. It is possible to plan a scale based on how low a commodity can go because of the practical floors built in. There is no absolute ceiling, however.

In 1995 cotton went to its highest price since the New York Cotton Exchange opened in 1870. Short scales can be suicidal. Imagine if you were short scaling before 1972. At that time the highest soybean price in history had been $3.75 per bushel. Suddenly Richard Nixon signs a grain deal with the Russians at a cheap price. That same season we have a drought in the Midwest. Boom! The price went to $12—more than four times the previous all-time high!

Don't get caught short! When a market is soaring, it tends to get very emotional. Everybody wants to buy in, and a lot of those buyers know nothing about what the price should be. They almost always drive the price to unrealistic highs before the market comes crashing down. On the other hand, when commodity markets drop to low prices, there is a tendency for everyone to lose interest. Volatility declines, both in percentage terms and in absolute dollar terms. Bottoms are rarely emotional, and although they may carry to unrealistically low prices due to the lack of buyers, the absence of volatility and emotion means that prices get overdone on the down-side less frequently and to a lesser degree than at market tops.

Be safe. There are lots of opportunities to scale at market bot-toms; leave those wild market tops to somebody else.

We now have our first principle for knowing when to scale. *Only scale at market lows, never at market tops.* Well, if we're going to be buying into market declines, we still need to know when to start. There are two tools at our disposal to help us determine when a declin-ing market is likely to bottom and start heading higher: (1) price charts, the study of which is known as technical analysis; and (2) fun-damental analysis, which is the study of supply-and-demand statistics. Because scale trading relies on the economic law of supply and de-mand, it follows that the scale trader should rely more heavily on fun-damental analysis than on technical analysis. This presents a problem, the solution for which we will be discussing at length in this book.

FUNDAMENTAL ANALYSIS

Technical analysis is done by almost everybody, and fundamental analysis is done by only a few. The reason for this lies not in the effec-tiveness of one over the other but in the availability of data and the ease of interpretation. Prices are broadcast constantly throughout the trading day by private data vendors who send them to customers via satellite, phone lines, cable hookups, or the Internet. The data are col-lected by thousands of computers around the world. Dozens of differ-ent software programs are available to convert this price data into charts and to then allow the trader or the analyst to manipulate the charts with studies such as the relative strength index, moving aver-ages, and trend lines to aid technical analysis. Technical analysis soft-ware programs automate many of these features, making technical analysis as simple (at least to do, if not to understand) as clicking a few buttons.

News affecting supply and demand is also broadcast throughout the day. The difference between the news and the price data is that price is in the form of numeric data that a computer can easily con-vert into a chart whereas supply and demand information is in the form of text (often with statistics buried in them). Computers often find it extremely difficult, if not impossible, to convert that informa-tion into a chart automatically. Therefore, the fundamental analyst must take some time to extract the statistics from news reports, government reports, and private reporting companies. Then the data must be converted into charts and/or tables for interpretation.

Technical analysis is a tool better suited to the fast pace of the trading world. In an instant you can display any market on your screen, do all sorts of studies on it, and reach an opinion. Figure 2.7 shows a price chart for crude oil with several technical indicators and market studies. Constructing this chart took a technical analyst all of 30 seconds.

By contrast, the fundamental analyst quietly ponders reports and data from various sources, written and electronic, before reaching conclusions about market direction. The vast majority of traders, large and small, don't have the inclination to do that. Hence, the popularity of technical analysis and, hence, the scale traders' problem.

If fundamental analysts are few and far between, then the scale trader faces the daunting task of becoming his or her own fundamental analyst or finding a good fundamental analyst on whom to rely. Becoming a good fundamental analyst is possible and potentially very rewarding. Finding a good fundamental analyst on whom you can count may be a good bit easier.

One way to have a good fundamental analyst is to have a full-service broker who has excellent fundamental information and

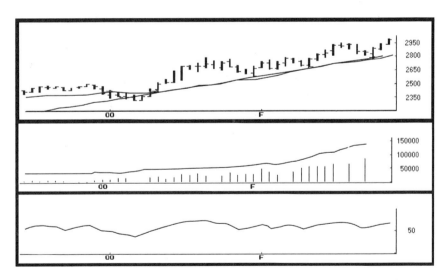

Figure 2.7 April 2000 crude oil futures with trendline and indicators. (*Source:* FutureSource/Bridge)

analysis available for your use. Some good brokers include this information as part of their brokerage service. It is for this reason and others that I recommend that scale traders use a full-service broker. In choosing among several brokers, take time to review what they have to offer in the area of fundamental analysis. If you can find a broker who will provide you with good fundamental information and analysis, you won't need to become a fundamental analyst yourself. Your problem will be solved.

Later, starting in Chapter 4, "Fundamentals the Right Way," I will lay out a primer for those of you who would like to do your own fundamental analysis. In the best of all worlds, scale traders would do their own fundamental analysis and at the same time have access to a broker knowledgeable in fundamental analysis who can be a quality partner in the scale trader's pursuit of excellence in trading.

BOTTOM THIRD OF TRADING RANGE

Although fundamentals—supply and demand—are the foundation of scale trading, it is very difficult to pinpoint exactly when a market is going to bottom using fundamentals alone. Fundamentals may help you form an opinion about when a market might be approaching a bottom, but a small amount of additional help is required from technical analysis. When used properly, price charts can be helpful. It is important to understand that price charts are only a secondary tool. Why will become clear in a moment.

One advantage of price charts is that they provide a succinct, easily understandable picture of the price history of a market, information that is always helpful to the fundamental analyst. Looking at Figure 2.2 again, you can clearly see that in the past 20 years any price between $5 and $6 for soybeans has represented good value. In almost every year during this period soybeans have managed to eventually get over $6. Does that mean you should automatically scale soybeans every time they are under $6? Absolutely not. Use price charts as a guide or as an early-warning system. When prices are approaching the bottom third of their historic trading range, you know it's time to check out the fundamentals. Fundamentals will ultimately decide whether the appropriate time has come to commence a scale.

It is important to make a few refinements about what we mean when we say the bottom third of the historic trading range. First, look over what has been going on in this commodity during the past

20 years, 10 years, 5 years, and 3 years. What we're looking for is a clearly defined notion of what the lower limits of this range are over a reasonably long period of time. There are no hard-and-fast rules on this. The price territory of commodities can change over time. If we go back too far, we may be looking at unrealistically low prices, such as pre-1972 soybeans. If we don't go back far enough, we may be looking at a trading range that doesn't go low enough. The goal is to get a grasp on how prices are likely to trade in the future by putting price action in its historical context. Try to filter out periods of abnormal price activity and extreme events.

Start looking at the longest time period and then work your way to the most recent period. Each commodity is different, and you must establish the correct period for each one. Cattle, for instance, began a very long term bull market in 1978. It would be a mistake to look at only the past 5 years in cattle. Soybeans, as previously discussed, moved to new high ground in 1972. Since 1972 they have not traded below $4. Prior to that time, they did not trade above $3.75. This is where experience comes in. Should you include price history before 1972 in deciding your trading range? I do not believe this is necessary. With experience you begin to learn to judge recent fundamentals in the context of the long-term range.

To establish what the bottom third of a trading range is, you also need to determine what the historic highs have been. This also requires some judgment and common sense on your part. In Figure 2.2, you will see several times when soybeans soared, for brief periods, to prices of $9 and higher. Should you include these spikes in your range? No. In the case of soybeans, every few years there is a drought in the Midwest. The severe reduction of supply caused by a drought sends the price of soybeans and grains soaring. But these highs are produced by an unusual circumstance—a drought. If you include these exceptionally high prices in your calculations, you will end up with too high a number for the bottom third of your trading range. I suggest you look at what the high end of the trading range normally is when there are no unusual events such as a drought for soybeans or a Middle East war for crude oil.

PATIENCE, PATIENCE

I have been involved in scale trading for years. During this time there has almost always been some commodity that was trading in the bottom third of its historic trading range. But even with all the markets from which to choose, it sometimes happens that no markets meet this criterion.

Now pay attention here. This is one of the most important things I can tell you: *If there is nothing out there that meets your criterion, don't trade.*

This seems to be simple enough advice, but I cannot tell you how many times I have seen people suffer unnecessary losses because of impatience. If there is one virtue that a scale trader needs in abundance more than any other, it is patience. You need patience when there is nothing to do but wait for the markets to come to you. You also need patience when you are in a scale. Sometimes you will enter a scale, begin your buying program, and find that the market goes down and down and down until it gets lower than the lowest price you figured it would get to—and still it goes lower. If you have planned and capitalized properly, this shouldn't be a problem, but the emotions can kill you. You need courage and patience at times like these.

I have repeatedly seen traders with accounts that had adequate financing to weather this type of storm, but they did not have adequate emotional fortitude. I have sadly witnessed many of these traders giving up and taking very large losses, only to see the market bottom a short time later and rally up to where they would have been profitable on all their positions. It is difficult to tell you that the most important thing to do in times like this is to hang on. The truth is that the market you are trading is perfectly capable of dropping to such a low price that your account could be wiped out, and you may even have to send additional money to your broker to cover deficits.

However, if you follow the guidelines in this book carefully, it is more than likely that the market will recover and that all will be wonderful and profitable, if only you can hang in there. Deciding to stick with it is a very tough decision that I don't want to make for you. The most important thing is to study and plan *before* you scale so that if you find yourself buried in a scale, you will have enough knowledge to help you know what to do. Most of the time—maybe even almost all the time—the right thing to do is going to be to stick it out. I assure you that you will find yourself in this situation sooner or later if you scale trade, so be prepared for it before it happens. Read carefully the sections of this book on planning and capitalization. If you fortify yourself financially and emotionally for these times, you'll probably be all right.

Even when you have carefully planned and carefully studied the fundamentals, things can change. This is unavoidable. It is important to stay abreast of changes in the fundamentals. You may find it necessary, as new fundamental information comes to light, to alter your plan. Perhaps you should buy contracts at less frequent intervals or maybe even suspend buying altogether. Keeping informed about fundamentals can help you decide when it is necessary to make these types of changes. I want to emphasize that the necessity for making these changes will be rare but still, it happens (I believe the epithet is "Shit happens").

All right, so you have identified a commodity that is either in the bottom third of its range or approaching it. As I mentioned before, do not begin buying it for this reason alone. You must check two things, and one is more important than the other. First you need to check the *fundamentals*. If you are satisfied that the fundamentals indicate that the commodity may be approaching a bottom, then it is a good idea to check the *seasonal tendencies* of this market.

There are so many misconceptions about fundamentals that I shall devote several chapters to them. Seasonals have been subject to so much misuse and misunderstanding that they also will have their own section. But because fundamentals are most important, they will come first, starting in Chapter 4.

3

WHY IS SCALE TRADING BETTER THAN OTHER TYPES OF TRADING?

If you have traded commodities, this chapter will likely reflect some of your experience. Like many people, you probably started trading with a great deal of enthusiasm and optimism, only to have your initial illusions smashed on the reality of the marketplace. We experienced commodity traders have discovered one truth that is almost universal among us: *Commodity trading is not easy,* especially if you have been doing most other things besides scale trading. If you have come to commodity trading by way of some of the popular books and courses currently available, this difficulty may come as a surprise to you. So I'd like to give you a very brief survey of commodity trading the way it is usually done by those who do not use scale trading.

In my nearly 15 years as a broker, I have handled hundreds of accounts and have witnessed the results of hundreds of other accounts handled by fellow brokers. When reviewing my experience with those accounts that have not utilized scale trading, they have largely been unprofitable, with only a few exceptions. It seems that almost any method other than scale trading doesn't work for very long, if at all. Thankfully, I have found some exceptions to that last statement, and I will direct you to a couple of those in Appendix II, "Other Possibly Profitable Methods."

I would like to ignore those exceptions for the moment and focus on why other types of trading have been so difficult and almost universally futile. Several things can help you understand why. First, recall our discussion of technical analysis in Chapter 2. Most traders and analysts—indeed, probably more than 90 percent—use technical rather than fundamental analysis. This means that almost everyone is looking at the same data. Now, they certainly do different things with it, but a chart is a chart is a chart. When hundreds and thousands of people are all looking at the same chart, only so many interpretations are possible.

To oversimplify for the moment, a market is bullish, bearish, or neutral. If the majority decide they are bullish, they will all buy and push the price of the market up. Most of the time they will push it too high. After everyone has bought, no more buyers are left, and the price will naturally begin to fall. This may occur gradually or all at once, depending on how many sellers appear. Of course, every seller must eventually find a buyer; but in the absence of an abundance of eager buyers, they will have to lower their price continuously to attract new buyers.

This means that all those people who bought after the prices had already started rising, including most trend followers, will start losing money as the price declines. If the price declines enough, new short sellers will enter the market, driving it ever lower until the longs either give up or reverse their positions to the short side, starting the process all over again. Now the chart has begun to look bearish, attracting the technical traders to the short side.

TREND FOLLOWING

Technical traders generally come in two types: trend followers and range traders. Trend followers make up the majority. They are the crowd followers. If the market is rising, buy it. If it is dropping, sell it. There are probably a thousand different ways to do this, but the object is the same: Get on the trend and ride it. Have you ever heard sayings like "The trend is your friend" and "Don't buck the trend"? These systems work very well at times. The lucky trend traders who bought cotton at 85 cents on its way to $1.14 (Figure 3.1) made a lot of money when you consider that every penny in cotton is worth $500.

A study of charts shows lots and lots of opportunities to catch a move like this and ride it. Our greed for profit encourages us to try to find something like that and ride it out. Looking at a chart like the cotton market in 1995, it's easy to understand why so many people

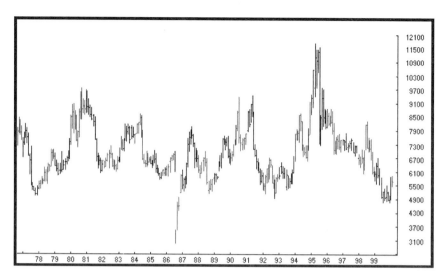

Figure 3.1 Monthly cotton chart. (*Source:* FutureSource/Bridge)

trend trade. In our dreams we buy near the lows, keep adding to our position, and somehow get out at just the right time with a million dollars in profit. Reality is usually something else.

Markets, unfortunately, trend far less often than they wander aimlessly or do nothing at all. As a result, the biggest drawback of trend-following systems is that they often take a long time to make money, and you have to put up with big losses on the way to your ultimate goal. Most traders don't have the patience or the pocketbook to stick with these methods.

Look at some charts. Look carefully and find times when a market looked as if it were starting to trend and then didn't. You'll have to look very carefully to find these instances. They're hard to see because what your eye is looking for is a trend. It's a lot harder to find the instances when a trend looks as if it's getting started and doesn't than it is to find the instances when a trend actually occurs. Look for a sideways market—a trading range where the price pops above or below the previous high or low of the sideways activity, only to fall back into the same sideways range without ever getting going one way or another.

I know of one famous trader who uses these trading ranges as the basis of his trading system. He waits for one to set up, and then, when it breaks out of the range, he will establish a position in the same direction as the breakout. In other words, if the market moves above the trading range, he will buy long. If it moves below the range, he will sell short. This is a very logical methodology. It is based on the concept that commodity prices try to find equilibrium. When they find that equilibrium, they will stay there until some demand or supply factor changes, causing an imbalance that will then cause the price to move quickly until it finds a new equilibrium level. In this model, prices spend most of their time in sideways consolidations with brief strong trends moving the price from one level to another. Because you need a change in prices to make money, the idea is to stay out of the sideways stuff, wait for one of those nice quick trends to occur, and then jump on it, trying to catch it as close to the beginning as possible. Sounds great, right?

Well, if you took the time to really study those charts I referred to earlier, you will find that markets frequently engage in a very nasty behavior called "false breakouts." Breakout traders hate these. They cost money. That famous trader I referred to earlier? His win/loss percentage is less than 40 percent, and it occasionally dips all the way down to 20 percent! I have found that it is a very rare individual indeed who will put up with losing money on 60 percent to 80 percent of their trades.

Look at your charts again. Find a small rally or a decline that reverses itself. When this move started, was it seen as a correction or as a trend reversal? Figures 3.2 and 3.3 provide excellent illustrations of this kind of price behavior.

When these little moves first occur, traders start getting into the market, hoping for a trend to follow, only to have the market back up on them and stop them out of their position with either minimal gains or losses (losses most of the time). These little false starts are perhaps the biggest reason why trend traders fail so often. As I mentioned earlier, false starts usually outnumber the real trends by a wide margin. The trend trader usually ends up with mounting losses and often wipes out his or her account before hitting a real trend.

Even when the trend trader hits a genuine trend, he or she will find that it's not so easy to hang on. When do you take your profits? Do you use a target that your technical analysis derives for you? What if the price greatly exceeds your target? You'll leave a lot of profit on the table that you could have had if you had only stayed in the position. Should you use a trailing stop instead? If you do, how wide a stop should you use?

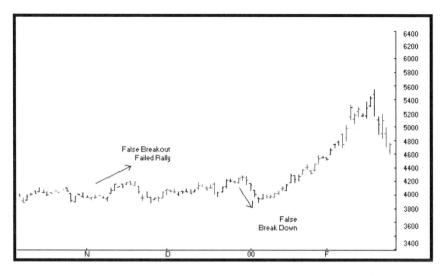

Figure 3.2 April 2000 platinum futures showing false signals. (*Source:* FutureSource/Bridge)

Figure 3.3 March 2000 Swiss franc futures showing false signals. (*Source:* FutureSource/Bridge)

STOPS

If you trade like most trend followers, once the trend has started you will use a *trailing stop*—one that you adjust continually with the advancing or declining price so you can lock in at least a portion of your profits. If you don't take profits at some target, your alternative is to keep moving your stop with the price action until the market reverses and takes you out of the trade by hitting your stop. This can be highly problematic. If you use a wide stop that is far from the price action, then when the market reverses, you will see a significant amount of profit lost before your stop is finally hit. If your stop is too tight, you will probably get stopped out of your trade long before the move has matured, and you risk missing out on a big trade. Stop placement is an art that is learned by trial and error over a long time. It is far from a perfect art, even for those with considerable experience. It is highly frustrating, and all too frequently you get stopped out of a trade with a loss, only to see the market go in the direction you had foreseen but without you!

Stops also have a built-in problem. What many people are not aware of is that getting stopped out of a trade is often something that has been engineered. It's not so hard to understand how this would happen. When you place a stop order, it is not unusual for your order to be either in front of or bunched together with lots of other trend followers' stops. Remember, everyone is looking at the same charts, so it should come as no surprise that a large number of stop orders would end up at the same place.

Professional traders on the floor, called *locals,* are aware of where the stops accumulate. It's supposed to be against the rules for that information to be circulated, but the locals know that the rule is often ignored. Whether or not the rule is enforced, everybody is looking at the same chart. If the market is not particularly active or if there is no new fundamental information to move the market one way or another, what often happens is that large traders begin to intentionally move the market toward the stops.

Suppose the cattle market has been trending up. Maybe the price has advanced from 6100 to 6400 over a period of 10 trading days. This advance has attracted more and more buyers who are now long and have a large number of stops placed just under 6325. If several large traders start taking profits and then go further and start selling short, they are often able to engineer a downmove. They'll keep selling, driving the price lower and attracting other sellers, until they find the sell stops at 6325.

Now all those trend followers' stops get hit. And guess what those large professional traders are doing? They're buying! Remember, for every seller there must be a buyer. While the chart-following trend followers are getting stopped out, their sell orders are being bought by the professional traders taking profits by buying back their short positions. Anyone who thinks this is far-fetched only needs to find a local who will talk about it. He or she will be able to confirm that this happens all the time. Stops protect you from losses, but, ironically, they are sometimes the very reason that a loss occurs.

In scale trading, we do not use stops. Lots of people will read this statement, and, despite everything I have just said about stops, will have a mild panic attack. If you are an experienced trader, it has been ingrained in you to use stops. Many writers of books and articles point out that you must keep your losses small. One of the worst things you can do as a trend trader is to let a loss grow until it becomes unmanageable. If you are trend trading or doing almost any other kind of trading, it is probably foolhardy not to use stops. Yet stops are often one of the reasons why most other methods fail.

In scale trading, stops have no role at all. The whole idea of scale trading is to accumulate contracts at progressively lower prices and then, when the market rallies again, sell this inventory of contracts at progressively higher prices for a profit. If you use stops, you will be stopped out of these contracts, and you will not have any inventory to sell at a profit.

If you use stops, instead of making a profit on almost every trade, the stops would insure that you have a loss on almost every trade. I know this flies in the face of common sense, but in scale trading you *must* accumulate large losses on your positions. After all, if you are going to acquire an inventory of contracts at progressively lower prices, the only way you can do it is if the contracts bought at the beginning of this program are held at a loss. To restate this boldly, you want to accumulate losing positions as a scale trader.

Let me repeat that: YOU WANT TO ACCUMULATE LOSING POSITIONS. There, that should get your attention. In scale trading, accumulating losing positions is the only way you can profit ultimately. It is the only way you can acquire your inventory. So, do not use stops in scale trading, please!

Scale trading avoids the pitfalls of trend trading. It avoids the problem of entering on false moves and being stopped out because of a wrong entry, a poor stop placement, or an engineered move. In scale trading, when the market is declining, the scale trader will be buying, often just at the time when all the trend traders are either selling a false breakdown or are getting stopped out of their long positions with a loss.

The reverse is true when a market is rallying. Scale traders sell into the rally rather than trying to buy more. As a result, it is hard to imagine a scale trader falling into the frustrating situation that many other traders find themselves in when they have bought the top or sold the bottom. It occasionally happens that scale traders actually sell the top and buy the bottom. I have always believed that this is the best and right way to trade: *Buy a falling market and sell into the rallies.* Scale trading gives me a method that makes this possible on a regular basis.

Technicians are plagued over and over again with false signals. Sometimes they buy a rising market, only to find they are in a trading range and have bought the top of the range. Hundreds of books, systems, and courses claim their brand of trend following makes money 70 percent or more of the time. Unfortunately, reality is quite different. Check out the *Commodity Traders Consumer Report* (CTCR). I have included a copy of a CTCR spread sheet showing the performance of 26 different newsletters (Figure 3.4). The report shows that few newsletters, if any, have years when they were right more than 60 percent of the time. In fact, only a few are right more than 50 percent of the time. This is reality. And remember, these guys are good enough to have a following.* Are you? If not, you may find your results considerably worse with trend following.

There are ways you may be able to make trend following work. The problem is that even with considerable capital and sophistication, getting more than about 55 percent winners is extremely difficult. In my experience as a broker I have found that most investors don't have the temperament required to be successful while being

---

*CTCR has a mixed criteria for selecting newsletters for review. CTCR thinks there are about 50 newsletters out there, and they review as many as possible. They select some simply because they are well-known; they look for a variety of methods; they don't review newsletters from brokerages; and the newsletters must give specific buy/sell instructions so that they are trackable.

Newsletter Track Records for September 1996

Vendor	% of Trades Profitable			Largest Drawdown in Monthly Net Gain (Loss) for the Past Twelve Months	Twelve-Month Net Gain as a Percent of "Reasonable" Margin
	Past Two Months	Past Six Months	Past Twelve Months		
1	33%	50%	64%	6,065	77%
2	43%	49%	55%	86,875	−24%
3	14%	43%	46%	7,675	−72%
4	56%	47%	50%	8,101	106%
5	50%	52%	53%	4,003	67%
6	57%	59%	na	884	3%
7	42%	42%	42%	22,872	−41%
8	24%	30%	31%	14,132	10%
9	60%	25%	23%	171,906	−99%
10	100%	35%	32%	245,675	−165%
11	22%	29%	22%	3,941	3%
12	22%	41%	37%	26,143	−64%
13	44%	34%	36%	59,405	−93%
14	50%	46%	46%	9,499	95%
15	58%	59%	63%	6,934	−13%
16	50%	40%	48%	6,330	105%
17	50%	39%	42%	834	−18%
18	23%	37%	38%	5,500	49%
19	0%	44%	46%	67,775	−17%
20	59%	57%	50%	19,057	52%
21	41%	47%	49%	1,775	7%
22	35%	33%	36%	57,126	−94%
23	20%	39%	38%	16,715	4%
24	0%	30%	39%	2,197	95%
25	42%	44%	42%	11,872	−5%
26	25%	19%	30%	11,787	−28%

Figure 3.4 This table reflects the most significant factors in CTCR's review of newsletters on the market as of September 1996. Due to regulatory and copyright restrictions, the vendors are not identified.

Definitions:

Profitable trades: The number of trades with a profit excluding commissions.

Largest drawdown in monthly net gain: An indication of the adviser's negative equity swings. CTCR uses only month-end equity change totals. Intramonth drawdowns may be larger.

Net gain (loss): The period's net change in account equality. It includes the change in open trade equity from the previous period plus the net closed profit or loss.

Return on "reasonable margin for yearly net gain/loss: The change in equity (net gain or loss) for the past 12 months divided by twice the maximum initial margin required. This category includes $80 per trade deducted for slippage and commissions.

CTCR's table was compiled from sources believed to be reliable, but the accuracy is not guaranteed. No representation can be made that future performance of any adviser will bear any relation to past performance. All reviews express only the opinion of CTCR. Trading futures is risky.

wrong 45 percent of the time—and that's at best. Being wrong that much means that you will have strings of losers that will run to as much as 10 trades or more; losing streaks of 3 to 5 trades are frequent, and drawdowns (cumulative losses) can be quite substantial.

New investors rarely have the capital or the emotional fortitude to continue an investment program that subjects them to so much financial and psychological adversity.

The fact of the matter is that even if investors have a very good trend-following method at their disposal, they are unlikely to have the courage to continue with it when experiencing the kind of losing streaks that are not unusual when you are wrong 45 percent of the time. Unless you have been in a position to work with it in a way that does not cost you money (such as computer testing or being a broker and trading it for customers so that you can absolutely verify that it works), it is unlikely that you will continue past the first couple of nasty drawdowns. Even when you have that kind of prior experience and knowledge with a system, it can be extremely difficult. After all, maybe this time is the time when this method will fail and take all your money with it.

TREND STABILITY VERSUS SENSITIVITY

A few things are common with these systems. They are based on charts. They are based on what the system did or would have done over a certain period of time. If it is a long period of time (i.e., 10 years or longer), it has the advantage of being a stable model. But it is a rare system that is both stable and sensitive. Stable models tend to be ones that allow the market considerable latitude. Latitude translates into risk. If you are going to give the market a lot of latitude, you are going to be taking a sizable risk. The risk is that the market will take all the latitude you have given it and keep going because your system was wrong. When this happens, you get stopped out with a large loss.

If the system was tested over a short period of time, you have another problem. It may be showing wonderful results because the market during the test period just happened to be favorable to your system. What happens when market conditions change and the new environment is not conducive to your system? You almost certainly will lose lots of money before you figure out that you are not just in a losing streak but that your system simply is not working in the new market environment.

There are lots of systems based on moving averages, stochastics, relative strength, William's %R, et cetera, et cetera. Lots more will be invented. These systems are, essentially, mathematical derivations of price action. They have a strong similarity to houses of cards: the more elaborate they become, the less likely they are to stand up.

To understand this better, you need to understand the principle of optimization. What people do in their search for the perfect system (often referred to as the search for the holy grail) is to create a system based on a certain set of data—1 year, 5 years, 10 years, and so on. After establishing that there may be something interesting, they optimize it—they find the particular parameters that will give them the optimal performance.

For instance, suppose you determined that a simple moving average worked pretty well in wheat. But what moving average—10-day? 11-day? 14-day? So typically a computer is employed to find the exact moving average that would have worked best over the test period. But that's only what worked best over the test period. Markets are in a constant state of flux. The morning may be different than the afternoon. If we can see different market characteristics within the same day, how much more difference will we see over a period of months and years? The answer is quite a lot.

Look at the January soybean charts for three years (Figures 3.5 to 3.7). The 1993 soybean market was quite different from the 1994 market, and the 1994 market was quite different from the 1995 market. The ideal moving average for 1993 would be different from the ideal moving average for 1994, and 1995's average would be different from that of 1994 and probably from that of 1993. Many people try to correct this by reoptimizing frequently. This is an attempt to change the system as the market changes. The problem is that all optimizations are based on data of past market activity.

Here we are getting to the crux of the difficulty in designing trading systems. No one can foretell the future. But we have to trade in the future, and the only guide we have is the past. I could spend a good part of the rest of this book discussing the pros and cons of numerous creative and sophisticated attempts to solve this problem. I think it is safe to say that the problem remains unsolved.

No one can predict the future based on the past. As Mark Twain said, "History never repeats itself, it only rhymes with itself." The fact

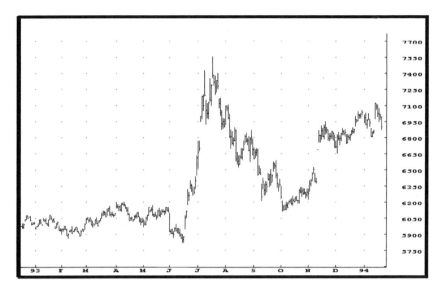

Figure 3.5   January 1994 soybeans. (*Source:* FutureSource/Bridge)

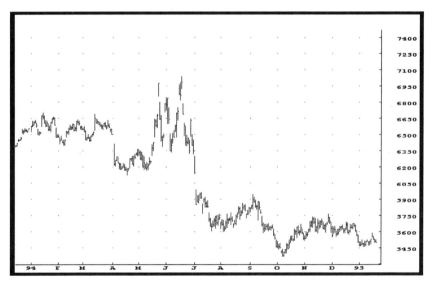

Figure 3.6   January 1995 soybeans. (*Source:* FutureSource/Bridge)

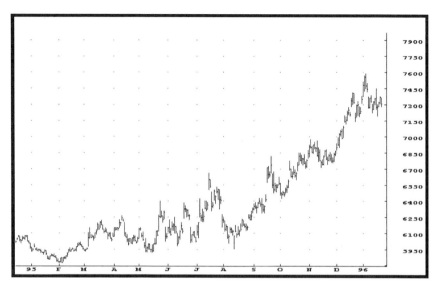

Figure 3.7   January 1996 soybeans. (*Source:* FutureSource/Bridge)

that it does rhyme with itself is why we can design trading systems that work at all. The fact that history does not repeat itself exactly (at least not usually) explains why it is so difficult to find consistently successful trading systems based on technical analysis.

Another problem deals with the degree of sophistication built into a technical trading method that is built on past data. The tendency is to look for something that works almost all of the time. The irony is that the more perfect the system, the less likely it is to continue to work. This irony is not hard to understand. Let's use an overly simple example. Suppose that the copper market went up for the first three trading days of March 1995. This could have been an entirely random occurrence. But further suppose, just coincidentally, that the market did the same thing in April. So your system becomes, "Buy on the last day of the month and take profits on the close of the third day." All right, you knew that wasn't going to work. But the point here is that optimization puts you in a position of having a system that is too rigid. In our case it was rigid about the time of the month. That inflexibility would cause us to trade the same way every month without consideration for other extenuating circumstances.

Computers can have the effect of making this problem worse. We can now have computers run over enormous quantities of data and try numerous variations on the same trading system in relatively short amounts of time. This allows us to create more elaborate structures. These houses of cards may work perfectly for the time period in our test data. As soon as we start trading them, however, we often find they don't work at all because the market has changed. The more elaborate they are, the more likely this is to occur.

Scale trading avoids these problems. It is a system based not on past data but rather on supply and demand. By keeping updated on changing fundamentals, you can easily adapt your scale plan to changing market conditions. It is not optimized. It is designed to buy low and sell high—buying low when prices are so depressed that the production is being cut back and selling high when prices are rising enough to attract new production.

PART **II**

LEARNING THE FUNDAMENTALS

This section explains what one of the most important components of scale trading, the fundamentals, is all about and how you can understand the key factors that affect prices in each market.

4

FUNDAMENTALS THE RIGHT WAY

Just what comprises fundamental research seems to be the area of greatest misunderstanding among investors. Fundamentals are not what we read in news reports. It is true that if we understand the fundamentals of a commodity, we will be able to interpret news events quickly and determine whether they have any meaning to our commodity. But it is also true that having no, or only a little, understanding of the fundamentals can lead to great mistakes about the meaning of news events. Many novice traders have lost their bankroll by trying to react to the constant flow of news. To protect themselves from this, many traders ignore news altogether. However, traders with a good understanding of fundamentals can use news to their advantage.

FUNDAMENTALS: WHAT THEY ARE AND ARE NOT

Fundamentals is the analysis of supply and demand. It is essentially a boring study of statistics. People who love to do this kind of work will please forgive me. Fortunately, a few people do love it and are good at it. If you, like me, are not crazy about this type of work, you must find someone who is. One of the difficulties you will encounter is that most of the really good fundamental analysts are not available to individual investors. A few newsletters do focus on fundamentals. A few brokerage houses also have in-house fundamental analysts. I have found one or two that appear to be useful. It is hard for me to give you some guidelines on selecting a good fundamental analyst.

The fact is that nothing succeeds like success. You need to follow these people for a while and see how they do.

As I hinted earlier, little or no knowledge of fundamentals can lead to lots of costly mistakes. As a broker, I repeatedly get calls from people who read *Investors' Business Daily* or the *Wall Street Journal* or watch CNBC. Naturally, many people who are interested in investing will look to get information from these and other financial news services. The problem is that, with little or no understanding of fundamentals they will learn of some important news and react to it in the wrong way at the wrong time.

News is not fundamentals. It is true that important news stories can impact fundamentals, and good fundamental analysts need to pay attention to the changing world. But the analysts can only assess the impact of the news if they first understand the supply-and-demand situation in the market they are following.

For instance, an investor may read that the wheat crop in Illinois is suffering from leaf rust, a type of fungus, and that wheat yields are going to be reduced drastically. In the same story, he may read that Indiana farmers are afraid of the same blight affecting them. Eager to capitalize on this information, he calls his broker and tells him to begin a scale in wheat. What the investor doesn't know is that Illinois wheat represents a very small percentage of the total wheat supply in the United States. A substantial yield loss in Illinois may be almost meaningless to the overall supply-and-demand fundamentals. Indeed, if Oklahoma and Kansas have had bumper crops, wheat may go down quite a bit after our investor has starting buying. What this investor doesn't know about wheat could fill a book and will probably cost him a great deal of money.

Consider my own experience in the stock market. In the fall of 1986 I heard on the radio that interest rates had just been lowered. I immediately called my broker and bought a large number of shares of various companies I was following. The next day the Dow dropped 86 points. At the time that was the largest one-day drop in history!

What happened? The market had already gone up a good deal in anticipation of the rate drop. In market terms, the market had already "discounted" the event. I was caught in an old situation called "Buy the rumor, sell the fact." Professional investors rushed to take the profits they had made during the advance the market had achieved prior to the rate decline. I was a victim of my own ignorance.

This situation represents another important factor in fundamental analysis. What is the right price, given the current fundamentals?

This takes considerable study by those wonderful people who love to study statistics (that is, not me). What they do is create tables (they love tables) of the average price in the past whenever these and other supply-and-demand situations have occurred. There are ways to do this work yourself, and I will recommend a book for you to read. However, if you're like me, find someone who will do this work for you.

The point you really need to know here is that it is not enough to know whether supply is tight or large; you also need to know whether the price is high or low, given that situation. To make things even more difficult, you not only need to know what the current supply-and-demand situation is, but you also need to be able to project how it will change.

Only with a good projection factored in can you truly know whether the market is overpriced or underpriced. This is because the current situation may be tight, and the market may appear to be underpriced based on that situation. However, if the projections are for supply to increase in the reasonably near future, the market will also focus on the coming increase in supply. The fundamentals are dynamic, and the market will try to anticipate the coming changes as well as to accommodate the current situation.

NEWS: A FEW THINGS YOU CAN USE

I hope I have frightened you into avoiding the classic mistake of reacting to news and partial information. Suppose you find yourself in the unfortunate position of not having access to really good fundamental research and are not able or willing to do the work yourself. I can give you a couple of things to look for in news or research reports to help you decide if the fundamentals might be ripe to begin a scale.

- *Price Range.* First, as we have mentioned before, you will have reviewed the long-term charts of the commodity and determined that the price is now either approaching or within the bottom third of its historic price range. You will have little need to confirm that the reason for this is due to an abundance of supply. Most likely, surpluses will be building, as occurred during the seven years that cocoa was overproduced from 1985 to 1991.

- *Evidence of Cutback.* Now, before committing to a scale, you must look for one critical piece of information. You must look for evidence of a cutback in production. As soon as you have that, in either government reports or news reports, you can begin your scale.

It is important that you do not scale before having evidence of a cutback in production. The example of changes in hog production will make this clear.

If you were to review hog charts for the past 10 years, you would find a lovely, exploitable pattern for scale traders. Every time hogs got down to 40 cents a pound, within a year to 18 months they were up to 55 to 60 cents a pound. Making money in this environment could not have been simpler for the scale trader. When hogs are 40 cents, the small farmers in Iowa, who produce 25 percent of the nation's hogs, have to cut back their production because their break-even point is between 42 and 46 cents. Small farmers are not blessed with the kind of capital it takes to weather such periods of price weakness. Eventually, this reduced production resulted in a shortage of supply, usually between 12 and 18 months out because of the growth cycle of hogs.

If, after having made good money from this for several years, a scale trader neglected to check for reports of cutbacks in production, in 1994 he would have paid a dear price for his neglect. Large corporations began to build big hog operations around the country. These large operations are far better financed than the family farmer. As a result, when prices dropped to 40 cents in 1994, the corporate farms kept producing at full capacity. The number of hogs coming to market actually grew at lower prices. This situation was exacerbated by the fact that the corporations, well aware that the family farmer cannot afford to produce at these price levels, expanded production aggressively to grab market share from those farmers who were forced to cut back production. So the price of hogs merrily went on down to 31 cents, destroying the accounts of those scale traders who had not done this one careful piece of homework.

Wait for reports of a cutback in production. At the end of 1994, with hog prices between 31 and 33 cents, the quarterly U.S. Department of Agriculture (USDA) Hogs and Pigs Report showed a decrease in the overall production for the coming quarters. For some time afterward, weekly slaughter numbers decreased by approximately 10 percent. Prices rose to approximately 40 cents, and continued to as high as 60 cents in 1997.

The scale trader who commenced his scale immediately after the December Hogs and Pigs Report would be a happy camper, unlike the scale trader who commenced his scale at 43 cents in the spring of 1994 only because this price level had worked very well in past years. Things change. Without a little careful study and planning, you can easily find yourself in a sorry pickle. But with the right information in your hands and with careful planning and execution, profitable trading is easily obtainable.

You may ask if the scale trader wouldn't have come out all right if he started at 43 cents and just held on until the price hopefully reached 50 cents. The answer is maybe—but maybe not. The hog market itself will create problems for him and so will the very structure of the futures market.

First, the hog market. Small farmers were forced to cut back production in large numbers due to low prices. Corporate farms were indeed very interested in taking market share in this environment, but they had some brakes put on their plans. Banks, seeing the low prices of hogs, were refusing to lend to corporations for the purpose of building new production facilities. Remember, nothing cures low prices like low prices.

But, as prices rose in 1995, more financing was available for the construction of new facilities, and the expansion by the corporate farms continued. By 1996 hog production expanded by some very large numbers. So the investor who bought hogs at 43 cents found that the market didn't get high enough to get him out as the market anticipated (remember, it is a "futures" market) the larger production expected in 1996. (It is important, however, to note that the 1994 market gurus were saying we would never see prices in the high 50s again. In 1996, due to production cutbacks brought on by the high price of corn, lo and behold, we did have prices that high. The moral for the scale trader is that it is probably better not to give up, even when things look pretty bleak.)

Second, the investor who bought at 43 cents in 1994 needs a much higher price than 43 cents in 1995. This is caused by that devil known as "carrying charges." Stay tuned—later when we pick up the discussion of carrying charges in the section on the dreaded rollovers.

DOING YOUR OWN ANALYSIS

For those of you who relish the idea of crunching numbers and reading government reports, you may want to try your hand at fundamental analysis. The reason is simple: By doing your own work, you can form your own opinion and not rely on someone else who may get it right, but, then again, may muck it up for you. In all commodities there are organizations that compile and publish supply-and-demand statistics. In the following chapters are outlines for each market group. First, an overview of what to look for if you are doing your own fundamental analysis:

- *Supply.* In all commodities, supply is basically made up of three categories:
  1. Surplus stocks left over from the year before (also known as carryin).
  2. This year's production.
  3. Any imports.
- *Demand.* Demand is made up of two categories:
  1. Domestic use.
  2. Any exports.
- *Carryout* (also known as ending stocks). This number is not difficult to obtain. Total up this year's supply from the carryin, this year's production, and any imports. Total up the demand from domestic use and exports. Subtract demand from supply, and you get the carryout.
- *Stocks-to-use ratio.* I like to look at the stocks-to-use ratio. This is simply the percentage of this year's ending stocks versus this year's use. For example, if this year's ending stocks in wheat were 900 million bushels and this year's usage totals 2.7 billion bushels, then your stocks-to-use ratio would be 33 percent. Most traders in the market key on the carryout figures of most commodities. There is nothing wrong with that, but I find the stocks-to-use ratio to be a better gauge because things change over time.

  In 1949 we used much less corn than today. A carryout of 1 billion bushels then would surely have sunk the market. But today a carryout of 1 billion bushels would not be an especially burdensome figure. What the stocks-to-use ratio tells you is just how tight supplies are. It tells you how much surplus we will carry into next year as insurance against production problems next season. A stocks-to-use ratio of 50 percent would be burdensome because we would be going into next year with half of our needs already met before we start producing. On the other hand, a stocks-to-use ratio of 10 percent would be of great concern because we would not have much margin for error. Any falloff in production of greater than 10 percent would create a shortage.

In the following chapters, I will outline specific sources of information and unique considerations for the various commodity groups. The comments here are only intended to get you started as a fundamental analyst and to illustrate how the fundamentals of each market segment might relate to scale trading. If you want to be a fundamental analyst, I suggest you obtain a copy of Jack Schwager's excellent book *The Complete Guide to the Futures Markets: Fundamental and Technical Analysis* (John Wiley & Sons, 1984). The first half of this tome is devoted to fundamental analysis. All the tools and skills you will need are there. This book is very academic and truly complete. Schwager also has published a more recent book, *Fundamental Analysis* (Ingram, 1996). I haven't read it, but given the excellent quality of his other books, I feel comfortable recommending it here.

5

GRAIN MARKET FUNDAMENTALS

The United States Department of Agriculture (USDA) is a great compiler of statistics and publishes them periodically for us. Every month the USDA publishes an updated balance sheet containing all the numbers you need to analyze these markets, including estimates of this year's production, exports, domestic use, carryout from last year, and expected carryout for this year. The USDA also publishes its estimates for production in the major foreign nations that either compete with U.S. producers for business, such as Brazil and Argentina, or are traditional importers, such as India, Russia, Pakistan, and Egypt. A monthly report on all grains comes out during the second week of the month at 7:30 A.M. central standard time. The exact date varies each month, so you need to check to see when it will be. The release of this report each month is a big event because it usually results in all the fundamental analysts checking their balance sheets to see if they either agree or disagree with the USDA's numbers.

During the week leading up to the USDA's monthly report, several private concerns release their estimates. The average of those estimates is what the market will expect in the USDA report. If the USDA's numbers differ greatly from the private reports, a price shock may occur in the market. For this reason, non–scale traders usually face significant event risk at the time of the USDA reports. The risk for scale traders is that the report comes out and proves that the assumptions that went into their decision to scale a particular commodity are wrong. If you ever find yourself in that unhappy situation, I suggest that you immediately take defensive action, such as that described in Chapter 14, and that you cease buying any more contracts until you get closer to your new target lows.

In addition to the monthly reports, the USDA issues two planting reports: (1) the Planting Intentions report, which comes out at the end of March, and (2) the final Acreage report, which comes out at the end of June and shows what farmers actually planted. The planting reports are important because they tell you a great deal about what you can expect for production in the coming year. When the Planting Intentions report comes out at the end of March, it can give you a head start on guesstimating this year's production. If acreage is declining this year, then we have what we are looking for—an expected decline in production. Before I would make a decision to scale, I would also want to know that the stocks-to-use ratio is forecast to decline and that prices are in the bottom third of their historical price range. If I had those two factors in place on March 31 and got a lower acreage number than a year ago, then I would want to scale that grain.

Very often what will happen is something like this: The USDA is forecasting a drop in the carryout in corn for the coming year. Then at the end of March the Planting Intentions report shows that farmers intend to plant less corn in the coming season than they did last year. What will then tend to happen is that corn prices will rise relative to soybean prices as corn attempts to "buy" acres away from soybeans before actual planting begins. At the end of June the USDA will tell us what actually happened. If prices were successful in "buying" acres from soybeans, then the revised acreage numbers in the June report will have a depressing effect on corn prices; if they were not, then corn prices will probably continue to rise.

As the year progresses, each month brings its monthly crop report and its associated drama. You must check each month to see that the general assumptions you have are still holding true, even as the USDA adjusts its figures monthly.

Each week also brings its own little drama. During the crop year the USDA releases a weekly report on crop progress and condition every Monday afternoon, on export inspections every Monday, and on export sales every Thursday morning. These reports give us clues as to how on target our assumptions are. If the weekly crop conditions report shows consistently high ratings, such as 90 percent good to excellent, then you can probably expect prices to fall toward, and maybe even below, the bottom of your scale. Most fundamental analysts keep a running total of the export sales to see how it compares to the USDA's estimate of annual sales. If sales fall too far off the pace necessary to meet the USDA's projections, then it is likely the USDA will lower those projections, thereby resulting in an increase in the carryout in the next monthly report.

When the USDA releases its Planting Intentions report and final Acreage report, it also releases its Grain Stocks report. This is an attempt by the USDA to tell us how much grain we actually have on hand. These numbers help confirm the accuracy of the carryout estimates in the USDA's monthly reports. In addition to the two Grain Stocks reports in March and June, the USDA also releases one at the end of September.

Finally, the USDA's monthly crop report in January is very important because, unlike the other 11 monthly reports, which are estimates, this one is supposed to have the final numbers for the previous year.

In addition to the USDA's reports, events that can impact prices may occur at any time. These may be the announcement of a large purchase by one of our export customers or the cancellation of a previous order or a weather-related event, such as a freeze on the winter wheat crop just before harvest. The fundamental analyst must watch these events unfold with an eye to the actual number of bushels that will be affected so that he or she may adjust his or her carryout estimate and, subsequently, the stocks-to-use ratio.

It is important to get actual bushel counts as quickly as possible to assess news events. For instance, a freeze of the winter wheat crop can be big news, sending prices flying higher. But if in the end only 1 million bushels is affected and if our carryout is 1 billion bushels, the final effect on prices is going to be negligible.

SOYBEAN COMPLEX

In addition to the general discussion about grains above, several factors affect each individual market. The soybean complex has three markets to consider along with the individual characteristics of beans: soybeans, meal, and oil.

Soybeans

First, let's look at beans themselves. When a crop is planted is an important consideration. Beans are planted in the spring, generally in April and May, but they can be planted as late as early July in the most extreme examples. A late-planted crop runs the risk of being caught by an early frost in the fall. A late-planted crop may have difficulty flowering and setting pods in the high heat of August. For these reasons a late-planted crop will generally command a higher weather premium than one that goes in the ground on a more timely basis.

How the crop comes to be planted late is another important consideration. In most parts of the country where soybeans are grown, corn is also grown. If the bean crop is going in the ground late because the corn crop went in the ground late, this may result in higher bean acreage. This is because corn has a longer growing season than beans so if farmers have trouble getting their corn crop in on time, they will often switch their last remaining acres to beans.

Through the summer, prices will often gyrate with the weather, especially at the critical times when the plant flowers and sets pods. It is important to keep from getting too caught up in the emotional drama of the summer bean market. Keep your eye on the monthly USDA figures, the weekly crop ratings, and the weekly export sales. If the weather turns hot and dry and prices soar, wish the trend followers well but remember something every farmer knows: Beans love hot, dry weather. Soybeans are known as the miracle plant because of their incredible resiliency. We do get droughts and we do get crop damage, but it takes severe weather problems for crop damage to happen. There's an old saying among farmers, "They kill the crop 10 times every year in Chicago."

Soybean Meal and Oil

As mentioned earlier, the bean market is actually three markets: beans, meal, and oil. When you crush a soybean, you get meal and oil. *Meal* makes up about 75 percent to 80 percent of the content of a bean. For that reason bean complex rallies are usually led by meal rather than oil. Meal is used for animal feed and is a direct competitor with corn. It is a higher quality protein than corn and, as such, commands a premium over corn. Factors affecting meal prices include the availability of meal from crushing operations; the price of fish meal, which is a competitor produced from anchovies fished off the Pacific coast of South America; the price of corn; and the size of the livestock herds.

Soybean *oil* is used mostly for cooking. Its competitors range from India's groundnut oil to Canada's canola oil, as well as rapeseed oil and sunflower oil. The most important competitor to soy oil is palm oil, mostly produced in Southeast Asia, particularly in Indonesia and Malaysia.

Each month the U.S. Census Bureau and the National Oil Processors Association (NOPA) release estimates of the crush rate and the stocks of meal and oil. The crush rate is an important factor in soybean demand, so these numbers are watched carefully. For instance, in late 1999 the crush rate was running at a record pace, but it fell off for a month. Demand for oil and meal did not drop, and as a result, stocks for both oil and meal showed up lower in the same report that showed the lower crush rate. This provides a pretty good clue that the crush rate will be going back up again to keep pace with demand.

Imbalances are frequent and interesting in this complex. If meal demand is huge and oil demand is not, then processors will crush at a furious pace to meet meal demand while oil stocks build up because oil is being created faster than it is being used. Because of these tendencies, spread trading between meal and oil is very popular and can work in the scale trader's favor. This can happen when an extreme imbalance has brought the price of one of these products very low. Traders have been making easy money on their spread, but now just about everyone is long one and short the other. As soon as the imbalance starts to be corrected, which is inevitable, the relationship between these markets can change with a vengeance. If the scale trader has been scaling the depressed product, then they could find themselves in the happy circumstance of having a number of contracts to sell in the panic rise that occurs as the spread unwinding panic ensues.

Bean Crops in Brazil

Prior to the 1970s, the United States was virtually the only place to buy beans and bean products. In the 1960s, at the request of President Lyndon Johnson, Dwayne Andreas, of Archer Daniels Midland, and others went to Brazil and taught the Brazilians to grow beans. Today Brazil and Argentina combine to produce as many soybeans as the United States does. Brazil has more than 200 million acres of uncultivated grasslands in central and northern Brazil that are ideal for bean crops. Until recently, this area was not thought to be good land, but now operations are getting as much as 50 bushels an acre there. These yields are on a par with U.S. yields.

Moving into the twenty-first century, the Brazilian government fully intends to see this area cultivated. This 200 million acres is equivalent to all of the corn and bean acreage in the U.S. heartland.

If Brazil is successful in developing this agricultural land for bean crops, then the growth of world demand for beans will be met easily—and then some. As a result, scale traders may have to revise their ideas of what low prices for beans are. As each year goes by, it should become more important to watch weather and production in Brazil.

CORN

Corn is a little simpler to watch than the soybean complex. Still, we have to watch more than just corn. The corn that is traded on the Chicago Board of Trade (CBOT) is animal feed, not the sweet corn you buy in the supermarket. The competitors of feed corn are feed wheat, sorghum, and bean meal. Foreign competitors are primarily China, South Africa, and Argentina. In recent years China has expanded its corn production aggressively so that it has gone from being a net importer to a net exporter of corn.

In general, corn is easier to kill than beans. It must be planted no later than mid-June, and even mid-June may be too late as late-planted corn will have to try to pollinate in the high heat of the summer in late July to mid-August. Late-planted corn is also vulnerable to an early frost in the fall. If corn gets planted late, farmers may switch to a variety that has a shorter growing season. If they do, these varieties tend toward lower yields.

Because half of the corn crop is used domestically, a fundamental analyst should keep an eye on livestock herd size to gauge feed usage. The most important numbers will be increases or decreases in the number of cattle on feed, the hog and pig crop, and poultry production.

Corn is also used in the production of sweeteners and ethanol. Ethanol production currently accounts for about 3 percent to 5 percent of all corn usage. It requires government subsidies to make it profitable. It is conceivable that production will grow in the future because of the lower emissions from ethanol, but it is a political issue that is hard to predict. It would be better if it were profitable to produce.

WHEAT

Wheat is the oldest commodity contract. It started trading in 1847 on the CBOT. It is food for humans as well as for animals. For many nations wheat is the dietary staple, and it is certainly a major part of the U.S. diet. For this reason, I have often pointed out that they were trading wheat on the CBOT before all the companies in the Dow were founded, and they will probably be trading it there after all those companies are out of business.

Kinds of Wheat

Wheat is traded on three different U.S. exchanges: (1) the CBOT, (2) the Kansas City Board of Trade (KCBOT), and (3) the Minneapolis Grain Exchange (MGE). *Chicago wheat* is soft winter wheat. It is planted in the fall and harvested in the late spring and early summer. It is grown primarily in the south-central Midwest states of Tennessee, Arkansas, Missouri and southern Illinois, Indiana, and Ohio. This is a low-grade wheat that is used mainly as animal feed and for flour for cheap bread or pizza dough. It is often exported to third-world countries because of its low price.

Kansas City wheat is the largest crop. It is hard, red, winter wheat and is grown in Texas, Oklahoma, Kansas, eastern Colorado, and southern Nebraska. This is prime bread and pizza dough wheat. About half of this crop gets exported. Like Chicago wheat, it is planted in the fall and harvested in the spring and summer. Chicago wheat and Kansas City wheat account for 60 percent to 75 percent of the wheat grown in the United States.

Minneapolis wheat is grown in the northern Plains states of Montana, the Dakotas, northern Nebraska, and Minnesota. This is the highest grade of wheat. It is known as spring wheat because it is planted in the spring and harvested in the fall. Pastry chefs prize this wheat, and there is often not enough of it. Because of this, it doesn't get exported very often, and it is occasionally blended with hard red winter wheat to make up enough quantity.

Global Wheat

Our competitors and customers in wheat pretty much make up the United Nations. Our competitors are most of the countries in Europe along with Argentina, Canada, and Australia. Our customers are just about everybody else, but in particular Egypt, Morocco, Pakistan, India, Russia, and China. Wheat is grown in almost every part of the globe, even Saudi Arabia. It is the first known crop to be cultivated by man. Iraq, which was Babylonia in ancient times, was the bread basket of the world in its time.

For some years now, we have been accustomed to looking at wheat in a global sense, whereas we tend to view corn and beans more parochially (though I strongly believe that situation will change over time so that we will view those markets much as we view the wheat market today). When the USDA provides us with its monthly estimates, it gives us two sets of numbers: one for all U.S. supply/demand and one for world supply/demand. In general, I suggest that you blend these two figures to come up with your stocks-to-use ratio and that you give a 60 percent weighting to the U.S. figures. This is a rough rule of thumb and has to be watched for times when it may need more or less weighting. For instance, in 1999 the southwestern United States was very dry, nearly a drought, but prices barely budged because of the abundance of wheat all over the world.

Wheat in the News

It is important to remember, as I keep stating, not to get carried away by news events. If you see news of a crop disaster, watch carefully for actual bushel figures and then see how these would affect your stocks-to-use ratio.

Wheat is a grass. Grass is hard to kill—my lawn always seems to come back, no matter how much it gets frozen in the winter or burned in the summer. It is possible to kill wheat, but it takes severe weather conditions to do it. Floods can kill it. Drought can kill it. Frost at the wrong time can kill it. But if drought or frost occur early enough in the growth cycle, wheat can recover fully with good weather the rest of the way to harvest. Perhaps most dangerous to the wheat crop is the loss of yields and quality if it gets too much rain right at the end of the crop cycle when it is time to harvest.

It may be outside of the realm of scale trading, but a good way to make money in wheat can occur when a late spring freeze sends prices soaring. If this happens, I recommend considering the purchase of put options as a speculative position.

PRICES AND STOCKS-TO-USE RATIOS

For most markets it is hard to come by good references that will lay out for you what to expect, given a particular stocks-to-use ratio. Fortunately, in grains we have such a reference. Before he passed away, William Grandmill produced a very useful book entitled *Investing in*

Wheat, Corn and Soybeans (Probus Financial Publishing, 1991). This book contains some very useful tables that you may use as a guide when determining what prices you should expect, given a certain stocks-to-use ratio.

In general, the way to arrive at these figures is the truly hard work of fundamental analysis. In short, it is necessary to obtain the stocks-to-use ratios for prior years. For agricultural markets, that information can be extracted from USDA archives, and for other markets, from their respective agencies. Once these numbers are obtained, a scatter plot is made of prices as they occurred with each stocks-to-use ratio level. From this diagram, you can derive price averages as well as price ranges.

6

LIVESTOCK MARKET FUNDAMENTALS

Unlike grain markets, where almost half of the use is exports, the livestock markets are much more domestic. Exports have become a more important factor in recent years but still only make up about 10 percent to 15 percent of total use. In at least one sense this gives us a little less to watch because we don't have to watch production and consumption in other countries. Prices for both cattle and hogs are almost exclusively influenced by domestic concerns.

The advance of agribusiness is very evident in the livestock markets. Packers have pushed more producers toward contract production—producers sell all of their production directly to the packer at a fixed price. This benefits producers, who know that they have a reliable outlet for their production and can make a reliable, if small, profit for their effort. It benefits the packer, who can avoid the vagaries of the livestock auction market. Contract production may eventually result in the demise of the livestock futures markets but not yet. Enough cattle and hogs are still auctioned on the open market to make futures contracts quite viable.

CATTLE

As with the grain markets, the livestock markets benefit from the reporting services of the U.S. Department of Agriculture (USDA). Once every month the USDA releases its Cattle-on-Feed report. In this report you can find most, if not all, of the information you need to construct your balance sheet.

59

As with all commodities, we are interested in the supply and the demand. In cattle these show up as the cattle on feed, the placements, and marketings. *Cattle on feed* represents the total number of cattle in feedlots. These cattle will be coming to market over the coming nine months, so this figure is broken down further by the number of cattle that have been on feed more than 120 days, more than 90 days, and so forth. The breakdown allows you to judge when these cattle will come to market. The total cattle-on-feed number is reported as a percentage of this year's supply against last year's (e.g., 95.6 percent). The total supply in absolute numbers is available in terms of the number of cattle slaughtered, the number on feed, and the tonnage of beef produced by the slaughter.

Placements is the number of cattle placed in feedlots, and *marketings* is the number of cattle marketed by these feedlots. In addition to these figures, the USDA reports the average weight of cattle brought to market each week, along with the total number slaughtered. Each day the USDA also reports the wholesale price of beef to retailers and the number of boxes sold. This provides a gauge of the strength of demand.

Each month the USDA also releases a cold storage report that includes all pork, beef, and orange juice in cold storage at various locations throughout the country. This figure is not as important to beef as it is to pork, but it is still important to include this number in your balance sheet.

At the end of January the USDA releases its annual cattle inventory report. This is important because it gives the best overall indication of what the supply is likely to be in the coming year. This report is one of the best indicators of whether the long-term trend in the cattle industry is toward increasing or decreasing production. This report includes the total number of calves and their ages. Calves generally come to the feedlots at about a year old, and they generally weigh a considerable amount when they get there. Feedlots finish off the feeding process that usually starts on pasture. If there is plentiful pasture, then calves will come to feedlots on the heavy side; if the pasture land is too dry, they will show up on the light side. Regardless of when they show up, the fact is that the total supply available in the coming year is very much determined by the number of calves. The only way to increase the number of calves significantly is to hold more cows out of the marketing cycle for them to breed. If this happens, then the current supply of market-ready animals will, at least temporarily, get tighter.

It would be nice if the supply were as easy to know as knowing the total number of calves and plotting out when they will be coming to market. Several variables make this difficult to do. The price of feed makes a big difference. If corn is cheap, feedlots tend to hold onto their animals longer and feed them cheap grain because they make more money on every additional pound the animals put on. This has the effect of distorting the flow of animals to market and, in the long run, increasing the total tonnage of beef. On the other hand, high-priced corn leads to animals coming to market a little lighter. And if corn prices get too high, as they do every few years, it often will lead to herd liquidation.

This is a situation every scale trader should watch for because it can be a golden opportunity. When the price of corn starts to approach $4 or more, it is often high enough to force some feedlots into bankruptcy. When a feedlot goes bankrupt, the bank takes over ownership of the cattle. Not being in the cattle business, banks immediately sell the herd they have just acquired. This tends to flood the market with large numbers of animals.

Furthermore, when feed is expensive, the market for calves dries up. Not only are some operators going out of business, but those remaining in business are not eager to acquire many calves to feed expensive corn. This puts pressure on calf-breeding operations, known as cow-calf operators. When cow-calf operators are forced into receivership because their market has dried up, the banks take the breeding stock and sell it all to the slaughterhouses. So you get a flood of market-ready animals, green cattle, and breeding stock all coming to market at once. This will normally collapse the market.

What happens next is interesting. In every case I have studied, the price of cattle will plunge until all this liquidation climaxes. A spike low forms, and then prices rocket up to a higher level than before the liquidation started. This is because the process of liquidation has sent many cows to market prematurely at lower-than-expected weights and it also has sent breeding stock to slaughter, thereby reducing the number of calves available in the future.

Because this tends to happen once every few years, scale traders in the cattle market should always plan their scales so they will be able to keep buying on the way down, realizing profits when a spike low is made and prices rocket to the upside. Take a look at the long-term charts for cattle (Figure 6.1). You can see that in 1988, 1994, and 1996 prices plunged, only to make a quick recovery.

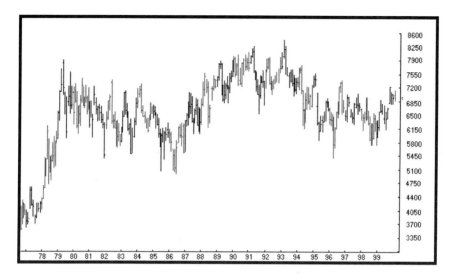

Figure 6.1 Monthly live cattle chart. (*Source:* FutureSource/Bridge)

Now look at the long-term corn chart (Figure 6.2). Note the years when cattle prices plunged and how they correspond to years when corn prices were approximately $3.25 or higher. In each of these instances, you can also see that the plunge was short-lived and that prices wound up higher than before the decline. This opportunity may only present itself every few years, but careful planning could result in substantial profits to scale traders as they acquire contracts on the way down and sell them at a profit on the way up.

The supply of cattle exhibits certain inelasticity in that it is at least partially determined by the population of calves. The demand for cattle is far more elastic. In good economic times people show a clear preference for beef, and consumption stays strong. If the world economy is strong, beef exports also will be strong. But beef consumption definitely suffers in a recession as many people will shift their diets toward the cheaper alternatives of pork and poultry. As a result, stock market plunges often affect livestock futures prices. The best way to keep a handle on cattle demand is to watch the monthly marketings number and, if you are inclined to watch the market everyday, to check the price and the volume of box beef sales. The price for "Choice" is a good proxy for the total box beef market.

One more point about cattle supply: Feedlot operators follow all the same factors that we do to plan when they will sell their cattle. If

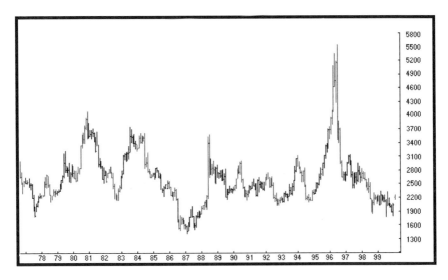

Figure 6.2 Monthly corn chart. (*Source:* FutureSource/Bridge)

the figures show that there will be a period when the number of available cattle will be tight, the tendency for producers will be to try to hold their cattle until that time frame so they can get a higher price for their animals. Likewise, if a period of plentiful supply appears to be coming, they will try to sell their cattle while prices are good. This is somewhat self-defeating and maddening to all involved because it has a tendency to take away the impending shortages or surpluses.

That this should happen should not come as a surprise to any experienced investor. Markets rarely advertise what is going to happen next. Markets at least try to be efficient and to discount the known. So you should expect that these impending events should at least occasionally be taken away. This should not affect the careful scale trader, who should be working off a balance sheet of total supply and demand and should not be trying to scale on the basis of short-term news, such as expectations for impending tight or plentiful supply.

FEEDER CATTLE

I personally find trading feeder cattle to be a little like playing the banjo. The guitar players among you who have tried to play the banjo will immediately relate to the feeling of confusion and chaos to which I am referring. Playing a nice orderly, logical instrument like the guitar and then moving to the wildly illogical and free-spirited banjo is a bit disconcerting. The feeder cattle market is not just another cattle market. To trade feeder cattle, you have to watch the feeder cattle market, the cattle market, and the corn market all at the same time. For this reason, I do not try to trade feeder cattle on a day-to-day basis. However, as a scale trader, there are times you might want to consider it.

The feeder cattle market is not as liquid as live cattle, so I would not want to choose it over scaling live cattle unless I found myself in the unusual circumstance of having high cattle prices and low feeder cattle prices. This would simply be an anomaly because if cattle prices were too high to scale, then the demand on the part of feedlots for calves should be strong enough to keep feeder cattle prices high, too. If you ever find that not to be the case, take a serious look at why calf prices are too low, and, based on that answer, consider if you want to scale feeder cattle. In general, however, I would not recommend this market for scaling because of its lack of liquidity, its lack of diversification from the more liquid live cattle market, and the more complicated analysis required to scale it.

HOGS

The cycle for hogs is significantly shorter than the cycle for cattle. Cattle gestate for approximately 284 days. Then the calves are started on grass or wheat pasture until they are no less than 600 pounds and as much as a year old before they get to the feed yard, where they may remain for as much as another seven to nine months. This makes it very difficult to change the number of market-ready cattle in a short period of time without disrupting the supply pipeline, as described previously, by holding back cattle for breeding.

On the other hand, it takes approximately 114 days to gestate a piglet and only about six months for the piglet to make it to market. That's about 290 days for hogs and a possible 860 days for cattle. This makes increases and decreases in production much easier to achieve. Because of this, the kind of sudden price downdrafts that occur in cattle can occur in hogs, but they are not always followed by the same dramatic price recoveries. What we saw in 1998 and 1999 was a collapse in prices during the fall of 1998 as the supply of market-ready hogs was more than the capacity of packing houses to handle them. Prices dropped on an inflation-adjusted basis to levels that were lower than those seen in the Great Depression. Full-grown hogs were fetching only about $20 a head! This had many long-term scale traders drooling—this is just the kind of opportunity they long for.

But it was not to be. Although front-month December 1998 futures fell to 20.23 cents per pound, the farther-out months were dramatically higher as the market discounted the industry's ability to change production levels rapidly. June and July 1999 hogs were actually trading at more than double the price of December 1998 futures as the end of 1998 neared. There was no opportunity to scale.

All the same, the shorter cycle in hogs can make this highly cyclical market a good scale trade candidate. Take a look at the long-term hog chart (Figure 6.3). You can see that spike down at the end of 1998 very clearly, but you can also see the rhythmic up-and-down price pattern in other years.

The USDA's quarterly Hogs and Pigs reports are chock full of important numbers regarding the nation's hog supply. But the fact that these reports are released only once every three months is often a problem for the marketplace. They are often subject to big changes from the previous report and are often at a large variance from analysts' expectations. Just take a look at what happened to July 1999

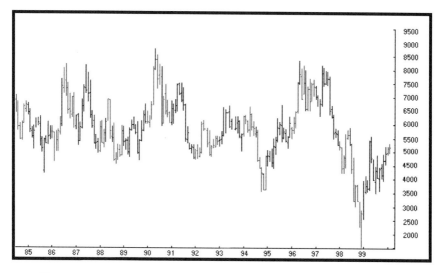

Figure 6.3 Monthly lean hogs chart. (*Source:* FutureSource/Bridge)

lean hog futures after the June 25, 1999, report (Figure 6.4). The market fell limit down for three days in a row.

On the one hand, these reports make scaling hogs a risky prospect because the government can come in and cut the legs out from under the assumptions you have been using to scale. On the other hand, taking a long-term perspective with the USDA's numbers can prove very rewarding.

For the scale trader the most important numbers in these quarterly reports are the "kept for breeding" number and the previous quarter's pig crop. These numbers will give you an idea of what the size of the production coming up will be. As with cattle, the numbers are given as percentages of last year's figures. If the kept-for-breeding number comes out at, say, 90 percent, you know that production for the coming quarter is likely to fall by 10 percent, a big number. Likewise, if the previous quarter's pig crop came out at 90 percent, a similar conclusion could be reached. As stated previously, the most important thing we are looking for as scale traders is evidence of a cutback in production. In hogs, that evidence will be found in the quarterly report.

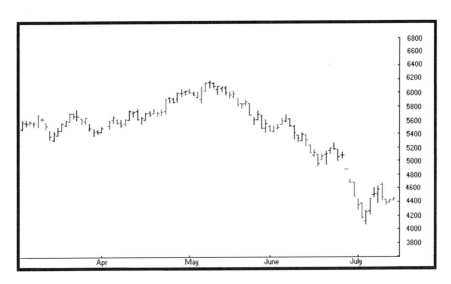

Figure 6.4   July 1999 lean hogs showing the impact of a bearish June hogs and pigs report. (*Source:* FutureSource/Bridge)

Another important report is the monthly cold storage report. This report shows the total weight of all commodities kept in cold storage, so it is important to the cattle, hog, pork belly, and frozen orange juice markets. The monthly cold storage report gives you the inventory of all the pork in cold storage. If production is coming down, then cold storage should also be coming down. Because this is a monthly rather than a quarterly report, it also can give you a clue as to which way the supply is going—up or down.

Wire services also report daily slaughter totals and cash prices for both hogs and cattle. These are fine to monitor, but, as daily figures, they should not figure much into the big-picture view that you need to have before deciding on whether to scale a market.

My ideal set of fundamentals for scaling hogs would be a huge supply reported to be in cold storage followed by a quarterly report showing a decline in the breeding stock and pig crop. If these fundamentals coincided with prices in the bottom third of the historical trading range for hogs, then I would proceed to set up a scale.

PORK BELLIES

Here is a notorious market if ever there was one. At least once a year it seems like I find myself at a party where someone asks me what I do for a living. When I say I'm in commodities, the predictable response is, "Ah, pork bellies." If you have traded long enough, I'm sure you've heard this as well. For some reason, futures trading has become synonymous with the infamous pork bellies. As most of us know, this is about as true as the idea that all landlords are like Snidley Whiplash of "Rocky and Bullwinkle" fame, who relishes throwing poor widows out on the street.

Pork bellies are the flanks and the ribs of the hog that are largely used to make bacon. With the popularity of the bacon cheeseburger and American's penchant for eating bacon on almost everything but ice cream, the demand for bellies in recent years has been phenomenal.

For the most part, I avoid pork bellies because of their violence. I know of no statistics on this, but I'm certain that pork bellies must make a daily limit move more often than any other commodity. This phenomenon can create tremendous opportunity if the scale trader is willing to capitalize one scale to such a high degree. In my career I have seen bellies trade in the 90-cent area and in the teens. I have seen bellies go up and down limit in the same day more than once.

This is a little challenging for most traders, but imagine how much money scale traders can make if they start the day by buying bellies on the way to down limit and then sell them on the way to limit up.

For most of you, the hog market will be volatile enough to create excitement. But for a few of you, the lure and excitement of bellies will be just what you are looking for. If you are that man or woman, keep reading. The quarterly Hogs and Pigs report is still going to be the most important single piece of fundamental news for you. This report gives you a gauge of the coming supply of hogs, and this represents the coming supply of bellies as well. Also of great importance to the belly market are the weekly and monthly cold storage reports, which allow you to follow the rise and fall of the supply of bellies in cold storage.

My ideal set of fundamental circumstances for pork bellies would be tight supplies of hogs combined with huge supplies of bellies and bellies trading at a discount to hog prices. My assumption would be that tight supplies of hogs would eventually translate into lower supplies of bellies in cold storage. I can monitor this each week with the cold storage report that gives me a net-in or net-out figure. In other words, did the supply of bellies in cold storage increase or decrease in the past week?

Normally, I stick to scaling hogs because they are volatile enough and are the primary market. But if that set of ideal circumstances were to surface, I would definitely consider a belly scale.

7

METALS MARKET FUNDAMENTALS

The biggest difference between the metals markets and other commodity markets is that metals are not perishable. This fundamental makes it hard to get shortages of any of the four major metals markets. Wheat that is consumed is gone forever. Silver can be recycled. All of the gold that has ever been mined in the history of the world is still available in some form.

This might make it seem like the supply of metals is essentially infinite. It is not. My gold wedding band might be available at some price, but at usual everyday prices for gold it is not. Each metal is like that. Large quantities could become available if prices were high enough, but they are not available at current prices. When silver went to $50 per ounce in 1980, we found out just how much silver could become available. A lot of silver tableware, jewelry, tea services, and so forth, became more valuable as bullion than as the items themselves and were melted down. Let's look at these markets one by one, starting with the most famous.

GOLD

Gold has been a symbol of wealth and value since the ancient Egyptians. For thousands of years it has been considered a storehouse of value, and until recently all the major currencies in the world were backed by gold. Originally, U.S. greenbacks were Treasury notes that could be exchanged for gold at any time. Because they were exchangeable for gold and because they are far more convenient to carry around than a pocketful of gold, paper notes became accepted as being as good as gold.

Demonetization of Gold

In recent decades gold has been undergoing a transition. It is slowly being demonetized. The paper money that was once used as a convenient substitute for gold has replaced gold altogether, even as paper money is being replaced by electronic bits. The history of this transition is very interesting. After World War II there was a meeting at a place in New Hampshire called Bretton Woods. The representatives of 44 countries met to establish the rules by which money could be exchanged, valued, and moved between countries. Their objective was to avoid competitive devaluations of the kind that had contributed to the Great Depression and to create an environment that would foster world economic growth. One of the mechanisms for doing this was to fix the exchange rates of the world's major currencies.

The agreement worked fine for some years, but by the 1970s it had begun to break down. As Richard Nixon's administration grappled with inflation, it took several drastic steps that included wage and price controls, among other things. One of the steps was to remove the dollar from the Bretton Woods accord and allow the dollar to float on the world market.

In the spirit of Bretton Woods, the United States had a law that restricted individuals from owning large amounts of foreign currency. The great economist John Maynard Keynes had made a considerable amount of money speculating on the exchange rates of various currencies. In the mid-1970s another famous economist, Milton Friedman, wrote a series of articles for *Business Week*. One of the subjects was his complaint that despite the fluctuations in the value of the dollar, U.S. citizens could not profit in the same way Keynes had by speculating on these value fluctuations.

A student from the University of Chicago who had sat in on some of Friedman's lectures thought he knew a way around the Bretton Woods accord. He was working as a summer intern at the Chicago Mercantile Exchange (CME) doing some clerical work. In those days the CME's big contracts were eggs and butter. It was known as the egg exchange and was a very distant second to the city's other great commodity exchange, the Chicago Board of Trade (CBOT). This student wondered whether a futures contract on currency exchange rates might be legal. He contacted Milton Friedman, who expressed the opinion that it might be. He discussed it with exchange officials, who were interested in trying it if he could assure them it was legal. He determined that it would take an opinion from the secretary of the treasury in Washington. He got a letter of introduction from Friedman and went to see Nixon's treasury secretary, who simply said, "If it's good enough for Milton, it's good enough for me."

What they didn't know was that the innocent persistence of a college student was about to change the financial world. In 1972, the first currency futures contracts were launched on the CME. The result was that U.S. citizens and corporations could now freely speculate on or hedge the fluctuation of the dollar on the world market. In time, this exception to the law brought an end to the law, and it was rescinded, allowing U.S. citizens and corporations to trade in currencies around the world.

With the simultaneous rise of technology, it soon became possible for anyone to move his or her money instantly from one country to another. This meant that the reasons to hold gold were obsolete. In the past whenever there has been concern about a currency, holders of that currency would revert to the gold that underlies the currency. The problem with that is that gold is cumbersome. Remember, it is this drawback of gold that led to the rise of paper money in the first place.

Gold has to be stored and insured. These things cost money. Currency, on the other hand, can earn money for the holder in the form of interest-earning deposits in foreign banks. Instead of going through the time-consuming and costly process of going to gold, the world's corporations and individuals have taken to shifting their money to what they deem as safer currencies in time of trouble. The two currencies that have seen the most of this kind of activity are the Swiss franc and the U.S. dollar. Switzerland, apart from being a nation of bankers, has not been involved in a war in nine hundred years. The fierce attachment of the Swiss to neutrality and their long history as the world's bankers foster faith that attracts the wealth of others from troubled parts of the world such as the Middle East and Russia.

The U.S. dollar represents the most powerful nation on earth, both militarily and economically. Some 90 percent of the world's commodities are priced in dollars, and most interbank transactions have dollars on one side of the transaction. The dollar is not just a safe haven; it is so deeply involved in the economies of so many countries that a few have even considered dropping their own currency and replacing it with U.S. dollars. After all, do you think more business in Moscow is done with rubles or with dollars?

The result of all of this is that the world's currencies have largely become paper-based currencies. Some argue that this is dangerous and that eventually we will need to return to the gold standard. I really don't know whether that is true or not, but what is undeniable is that the world is not on a gold standard now. Gold is being demonetized. Even the Swiss are recognizing this and are planning to sell some of their gold.

Gold Supplies

One result of the demonetization of gold is that the world's central banks are now holding enormous quantities of gold for which they have no need. It is a nonperforming asset and costs money to store, guard, and insure. This is a major concern to anyone considering scaling gold because the world's central banks hold an amount of gold in their vaults that is equal to ten times the world's annual mine production. All through the 1990s the world's central banks have been net sellers of gold, and I see no reason for this to change in the foreseeable future.

Given the low price of gold in recent years, it is no surprise that mine production has been coming down. Given the demonetization of gold and the tonnage that central banks would like to sell, it seems likely that production will continue to come down for years. Although there are very good political reasons for the price of gold to be kept high enough to keep the world's miners employed, there do not seem to be many purely economic reasons to mine as much gold as we do in a world where the central banks would like to divest themselves of so much.

The Gold Balance Sheet

Still, gold has five thousand years of history as a store of value. Some of you will read what I have written and ignore it because you don't believe that five thousand years of history will just go away. You certainly could be right, and so, for that reason, here are the factors you need to watch in gold.

As I have discussed elsewhere in this book, when considering supply and demand, consider supply first. It is usually the hardest to change and, therefore, the more reliable of the two. When constructing a gold balance sheet, the *supply side of the sheet* is made up of mine production, recycled/scrap, official sector sales, net disinvestment, and net producer hedging.

To plug these into your balance sheet, you'll need to come up with the data. A couple of places to check on the web are the World Gold Council at www.gold.org and Christian Precious Metals at www.cpmgroup.com.

Mine production is pretty clear. It is simply the total brought out of the ground from the world's mines. *Recycling/scrap* is also clear.

The other categories can use a little explanation. *Official sector sales* refers to the total of all governmental sales, such as from the Defense Department, the International Monetary Fund, the World Bank, and the world's central banks. Clearly, central bank sales make up the bulk of this category. *Net disinvestment* refers to the amount of coinage and investment gold sold minus the amount bought this year. This is kind of a toggle deal—if there is net disinvestment, it shows up as supply; if there is net investment, it shows up on the demand side of the balance sheet. *Net producer hedging* refers to the amount of forward sales by mines.

The *demand side of the balance sheet* is a little simpler. Fabrication is split between jewelry and other industrial usage, such as electronics. Then there is gold bar hoarding and net investment.

As with all commodities, the most important figures come from the bottom line. How much gold will be carried over into next year and what percentage of a year's supply does that represent? In other words, the most important figure will always be the stocks-to-use ratio.

SILVER

Demonetization of Silver

The demonetization of silver has been largely complete for a very long time. At one time U.S. dollar bills said they were "silver certificates," but that was done away with under Nixon. Hundreds of years ago the British pound was a note that could be exchanged for a pound of sterling silver. The currency may still be called the pound, but it has nothing to do with silver anymore. When I was young, I remember dimes and quarters made wholly out of silver. That is no longer the case. You can buy silver coins from the U.S. mint called American

Eagles, but I challenge anyone to use them as money. Can you imagine walking into the local grocery chain store and trying to buy groceries with American Eagle silver coins? The store would have no idea what they were worth.

Silver Supplies

Silver, like gold, is quite plentiful throughout the world. The supply of silver is so plentiful that few of the world's silver mines need to operate today. Because silver is plentiful even without the world's mines operating and because it has been demonetized, it seems very unlikely that we will ever see the kind of prices we saw in 1980 when the Hunt brothers tried to corner the market and sent prices to $50 per ounce.

Silver comes out of the ground from silver mines, but about 75 percent of the world's silver production is actually a by-product of copper, lead and gold mining. This makes the cost of production very low.

Bulls often like to point to the fact that for the past decade the world has consumed more silver than has been produced from mines. This is true, but there is a very good reason why the price has generally declined during that period. We have abundant existing supplies of silver. When the bulls point to the fact that demand exceeds mine production, they ignore the other sources of silver supply. In 1998 mine production represented only approximately 65 percent of total supply. About 22 percent came from recycling, 6 percent from "official sector" sales, and the remaining 7 percent from private sector coin and bullion sales. Looking at the total picture, demand has to exceed mine production by a considerable amount before the supply of silver would actually contract.

Digging deeper into these figures, if approximately 75 percent of the world's silver mine production is a by-product of other mining operations, then about 48 percent of the world's silver is going to be mined no matter what—it is essentially free. This makes it very difficult to put a low end of value for scaling silver because we know that even if it did go to zero, a substantial amount would still be produced. Even so, it is pretty hard to make a case for zero value to silver. It is used for jewelry, silverware, electronics, photographic film, x-ray film, and so forth. Although photographic demand has been climbing, its future is uncertain with the onset of digital cameras. On the other hand, electronics demand is one of the largest uses and is growing fast.

Over the long term, one big worry about silver is India. India is by far the largest consuming nation of silver because India is one of the few places where silver still counts as money. The people of India have little faith in their banks, so the average man on the street wears his life savings on his person in the form of leg and arm bracelets made from silver. It is true that India is one of the poorest nations in the world and that the average person's life savings do not amount to very much by Western standards. Remember, however, that there are approximately 1.2 billion Indians. No one knows for sure how much silver they are wearing, but some estimate that it is in the neighborhood of a trillion ounces. So the big question is what would happen with all that silver if India went through a cultural change and the average person started using checking accounts like we do. Fortunately, cultural changes, especially in India, occur slowly. So I think the scale trader can sleep safely at night without worrying that his or her scale is going to get buried by a trillion ounces of Indian silver.

The Silver Balance Sheet

The best source for gathering the information you will need for a balance sheet on silver is The Gold and Silver Institute in Washington, D.C. The Institute can be contacted at (202) 835-0185. Once per year it brings out all the data any fundamental analyst could want, but unfortunately, that is only once per year.

The rest of the year you have to monitor various trends to see how things are shaping up against your balance sheet. The most widely followed piece of information is the Comex Warehouse Stocks. The amount of silver, gold, and copper that the Comex in New York is holding in its warehouse for delivery on contracts is used as a proxy for whether the current supply is tight or plentiful. This is only a very rough gauge, at best, but still the trends of the amount of metal moving into and out of the Comex can at least give you a feel for what is going on in the cash market.

COPPER

Supplies

Copper is mined and used almost everywhere. The big producers are Chile and other Latin American countries, along with Indonesia and the United States. Chile produces almost 25 percent of the world's copper supply. From a scale trader's perspective, this is unfortunate. The usual response of most producers to low prices is to produce less as production becomes less profitable. In the case of Chile, the opposite occurs. The Chilean government owns a lot of the production, so when prices drop, so do governmental revenues. Officials usually increase production to make up for the revenue shortfall rather than decrease production. Also, it is very difficult politically for government-owned mines to reduce production because that means very unpopular layoffs.

When prices rise, Chilean workers usually will demand a cutback in hours along with an increase in wages. This will often result in a strike; so a rise in prices often has the effect of reducing production initially. As a result, copper prices are subject to accentuated extremes (Figure 7.1).

Demand

The demand side of copper is interesting because it is a very good barometer of world economic health. The use of copper is pretty constant from country to country when viewed as a percentage of Gross Domestic Product (GDP). It turns out that whether we are looking at

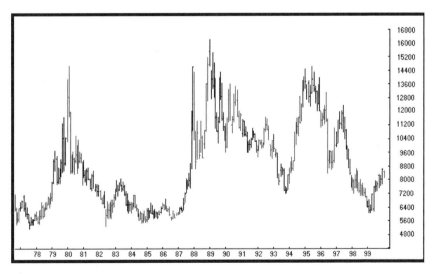

Figure 7.1 Monthly copper chart. (*Source:* FutureSource/Bridge)

Botswana or Japan, the use of copper will be about the same as a percentage of GDP. So one factor to watch in copper is the total world economic condition. When the Asian crises hit in November 1997, the result was a dramatic decline in copper prices because of the dramatic slowdown in economic activity in most of the world. This occurred at a time when the U.S. economy was very strong, so it is world economy, rather than the U.S. economy alone, that must be watched.

For statistics to fill in your balance sheet, I recommend The International Copper Study Group, which can be found on the Internet at www.icsg.org.

PLATINUM

Supplies

Of all of the precious metals traded, this is the only one that is truly rare. There are only three operating mines in the world. One is the Norilsk mine in Siberia; the other two are the Rustenberg and Impala mines in South Africa. These three mines produce approximately 75 percent of the world's platinum. The remainder comes out of the ground as a by-product of gold and nickel mining. When by-product production is added to the picture, the combination of production from Russia and South Africa adds up to 95 percent of the world's production.

Under the Soviets, Russia had a large stockpile of platinum for strategic purposes because of platinum's electronics uses. After the coup in 1992, the Yeltsin government sold off the entire stockpile, along with massive quantities of gold and silver, to raise hard currency. Russia shipped regularly from 1993 through 1996, thoroughly depressing the price down to 1991 recession levels.

Since then, Russian shipments have become increasingly infrequent. They did not ship from December 1996 through July 1997. Shipments then ceased again in December 1997 and did not resume until October 1998. They are shipping a little more now but not nearly enough to meet world demand.

Clearly, one important fundamental to follow is Russian shipments. Russia accounted for a little more than 25 percent of the world's supply until shipments ceased. The eventual resumption of those shipments should have at least a temporary depressing effect on prices.

What is also uncertain is when, if ever, the Russians will become reliable suppliers. I think it will be quite some time before that happens. The Soviets invested in Siberia. They built infrastructure and encouraged settlement. Each year they supplied Siberia with food and fuel before the long winter set in, and their military kept the railroad functioning.

Under the new regime Siberia has been in a state of collapse as the Yeltsin government focused on Moscow and immediate political and economic concerns and essentially abandoned the Soviet Siberia program as too expensive. As a result, many Siberian towns are down to 10 percent of their former populations, and the infrastructure does not function at all in the winter.

Keeping the massive Norilsk mining concern operational under these conditions has been close to impossible. Even if the new government in 2000 decided to reverse the abandonment of Siberia to better exploit the vast resources there, it would likely take years to rebuild from the damage that has been done by close to a decade of neglect.

Demand

Although the supply side of platinum struggles with Russian problems and a lack of meaningful supplies elsewhere, the demand side continues to expand. About 45 percent of the world's platinum is used for automobile catalytic converters, which are used in the United States, Japan, and Europe. The third world, though plagued with air pollution, has not yet implemented emission-reducing regulations. One would hope that someday the Mexicans would tire of the difficulty they have breathing in Mexico City; but, so far, poor air quality has not been enough to convince them of the worth of the additional cost of a car's catalytic converter. Should Mexico or Brazil or Indonesia or any other large developing nation start requiring catalytic converters, the price of platinum could soar.

About 45 percent of the world's platinum is used for jewelry. Of this about 90 percent is in Japan. Although most of the world prizes gold jewelry and uses gold wedding bands, the metal of choice for the average Japanese is platinum. A great deal of the growth in platinum demand has been coming from China and the United States as platinum jewelry is gaining in prestige for the high-end market. Both China and the United States have been experiencing double-digit percentage growth in platinum jewelry demand over the past couple of years.

The last 10 percent or so of demand is dominated by electronics use. This category is growing quickly as well. The growth in world demand has been so strong that total world demand continued to grow even while Japanese demand diminished from 1996 through 1998.

The Platinum Balance Sheet

The best source for your balance sheet information for platinum is Johnson Matthey. It is the world's largest distributor of platinum and releases an annual report on the industry. The company can be contacted at its Web site at www.johnsonmatthey.com or at (610) 971-3000.

Another useful source for metals information is the CPM Group, which can be found on the Internet at www.CPMGroup.com or in New York City at (212) 785-8320. The company offers a comprehensive fundamental report for a nominal fee.

8

ENERGY MARKET FUNDAMENTALS

In this category we have the crude oil complex and natural gas. The electrical power market is not recommended for scale trading as it is neither widely analyzed nor widely traded.

CRUDE OIL

Crude oil is the largest U.S. import. It is priced in dollars per barrel. It used to be considered a limited resource that was about to run out. Because it comes out of the earth, its supply is almost certainly limited, but the amount has been proving to be much larger than anyone had thought previously. The exploitation of the Caspian basin promises to keep the world well oiled for some time to come.

The supply of crude oil has become much more a political thing than a matter of economics. When prices were languishing at about $11 per barrel in early 1999, the oil ministers of the Organization of Petroleum Exporting Countries (OPEC) got together with some of their non-OPEC counterparts and forged an agreement to cut back production. That will last only so long before enough exceptions are made, either legally or otherwise, for the agreement to be no longer effective.

The political nature of the flow of oil makes for occasional sudden changes in that flow. The fact that reducing oil flow is simple to do also contributes to these sudden changes. Production is not so easy to slow down for other commodities. Even in a centrally planned economy—

China being the last major one, where it could be decided, for instance, to reduce wheat production next year—it will still take until next season for the effect of reduced production to be felt.

No such lag time occurs with oil production. The oil facilities just turn off the pumps. Presto! Oil production is reduced.

The demand side of oil is very much related to world economic health. Heating oil demand is fairly constant. Because oil heat is not installed as a rule in new installations, the amount of heating oil used each year does not tend to grow and is, of course, quite subject to the weather. Recessions do not tend to depress heating oil demand because we still need to keep warm. It is an essential, like food, that does not get cut back in hard times. Industrial demand is also fairly constant. Manufacturing concerns in the United States are among the most energy efficient in the world, so recession does not tend to affect industrial demand much.

UNLEADED GASOLINE

Unleaded gasoline is another story. The long-running growth cycle in the U.S. economy has led to a lack of consumer concern about automotive fuel efficiency. Americans whose wealth is increasing have been buying ever more sport utility vehicles that use ever more copious amounts of gas. Abroad, the growth of the world economy is tending to show up in the growth of auto ownership, particularly in developing nations in Asia. The overall effect is that, with the exception of the Asian contraction of 1998 and 1999, demand for unleaded gas has shown steady year-on-year growth.

The best thing for a scale trader to do is to wait for very low prices that are clearly producing economic pain for the third world countries that depend so heavily on oil production, such as Venezuela, Mexico, Indonesia, the Middle Eastern nations, and Russia.

ENERGY STATISTICS

You can follow the supply-and-demand statistics in the weekly American Petroleum Institute reports, which give the amount of gas, heating oil, and crude oil in storage and how much each is up or down from the previous week. The best reports are published by the Department of Energy in Washington, D.C. Like the reports of the U.S.

Department of Agriculture (USDA) for grains, these reports will provide all the information you need for your energy balance sheet. The Energy Information Agency can be found at www.eia.doe.gov. While you are on the Web, you might mosey over to the BP Amoco site, which publishes a good deal of statistical information on energies in Microsoft Excel format so you can just cut and paste it onto your own spread sheet. Pretty handy! The URL is www.bpamoco.com.

Some very good seasonal tendencies can be utilized in this complex. Crude oil prices tend to be low in the summer and around the turn of the year. This is because refineries produce products in advance of the season in which they are used. Heating oil buying tends to start in August, and most of the heating oil gets sold to jobbers for the coming winter by October or by November at the latest. Jobbers don't start buying unleaded gasoline for the coming driving season until sometime in February. That buying lasts until May. After those typical cutoff dates, only fill-in buying can boost prices. This often will produce a bump-up in prices right at the end of a cycle.

In April and November refineries shut down for two weeks for what is called changeover, a time when refineries clean facilities that have been used for the production of one product to switch over to the other product. So in April they clean heating oil facilities to change over to unleaded gasoline and then they reverse that process in November. It seems like in most years one last cold shot occurs after changeover and puts pressure on heating oil supplies in the spring. Then in November it often seems, particularly in recent years, that the weather is warmer than expected in the fall and, consequently, more unleaded was needed.

These bump-ups are fairly reliable, but I would not plan to use them for scale trading. Rather, I would use the broader tendency for jobbers to buy unleaded in the spring and heating oil in the fall. So, if unleaded were historically cheap in February, I could get interested in digging deeper into fundamentals to see if it were a viable scale candidate.

9

SOFTS MARKET FUNDAMENTALS

The softs group is an odd mix. It is often referred to as "tropicals" because these commodities are grown primarily in tropical or subtropical regions. In most cases, these are third world countries, which makes information a little unreliable and occasionally hard to come by. Each of these markets is unique and has different considerations.

COCOA

The cocoa bean comes from a tree. Because it grows on trees, changes in production occur over very long cycles. New trees take approximately seven years to mature and bear fruit. This makes production gains difficult to get quickly. But it makes it easy to forecast because the trees will have been planted years before.

Production cutbacks are not quite so hard to realize. If prices get too low, cocoa farmers will simply abandon marginal groves or just not spend the money on maintaining them. This is what happened in the early 1990s when prices reached down to $795 a tonne after having been at $4,500 a tonne back in 1976; the seventh consecutive year of overproduction was 1991. (A *tonne* is a metric ton equal to 1.1 U.S. tons.) The drop in price encouraged many farmers to abandon their groves, and a multiyear advance started. After the lows were made in 1992 the market rallied until 1999, when prices topped out at $1,787, more than double the 1992 low.

As of early 2000, cocoa production is expanding as a result of trees that were planted as prices began to rise again in the early 1990s and are now coming into production. The Ivory Coast, by far the biggest cocoa-growing nation, has achieved record-high production levels recently.

Cocoa statistics are released every year by the International Cocoa Organization (ICCO) at its annual conference in London. Several private organizations release their own estimates. The most widely followed is the F. O. Licht Company.

Measuring demand is a bit dicey. Throughout the year chocolate manufacturers release their cocoa grind statistics country by country. These grind statistics are taken as a proxy for demand. The problem with that is that more and more cocoa is being ground in the producing countries and shipped as cake, resulting in a decline in grind figures that probably does not represent a decline in overall demand.

In general, I have found that following the statistics of the F. O. Licht Company and the ICCO plus following trends on tree plantings in the major growing nations has been the best way to get a handle on cocoa fundamentals. As with other commodities, the stocks-to-use figure is your most important figure.

Recently, I was reading an airline magazine article about cocoa, and it brings up the importance of relying on your own work as much as possible. The magazine writer had heard that cocoa could be grown only in the shadow of the rain forest and that, with the rain forests around the world being burned, less and less land was available for cocoa groves. As a result, this writer forecast coming chocolate shortages. He wrote well and interviewed supposedly knowledgeable people, but he totally misled his readers. I'm sure it was all unintentional, but it serves as a reminder that, before putting your money on fantasies in the popular press, check out the statistics. Indonesia and West Africa are expanding production, and there are no shortages or forecast shortages of cocoa anywhere in the world.

One more thing that can, at least temporarily, influence prices can sometimes be hidden. Cocoa is priced in British pounds on the world market. This makes it somewhat unique because most other commodities are priced in U.S. dollars. The result is that if the British pound gets wildly divergent from its normal relationship to the dollar, it may stimulate or curtail cocoa export activity. This is usually just a short-term phenomenon, and I would not let it enter into my scale trade considerations.

COFFEE

This tropical crop is grown in so many different varieties that the Coffee, Sugar, and Cocoa Division of the New York Board of Trade has a scale that determines the ratio at which most varieties of coffee can be delivered against the contract there. The main division, however, is between African coffee, which is arabica coffee, and Latin American coffee, which is robusta coffee. The London coffee contract is arabica, and the New York contract is robusta. The United States imports robusta coffee almost exclusively. Coffee is the second largest U.S. import and until the 1960s it was the largest import; so this is a very important market. It is also a market subject to dramatic price volatility, which can make the careful, well-financed scale trader a great deal of money. Should you decide to scale this wild market, be advised that it is subject to extreme price swings that could easily eat your account whole if you are not adequately financed or if you run into some problem that your fundamental analysis did not foresee.

Coffee is grown on a bush. It takes three to five years for new bushes to mature sufficiently to produce fruit. Brazil is by far the largest robusta producer, followed by Colombia, Ecuador, Costa Rica, and other Latin American countries.

The International Coffee Organization (ICO) is a consortium of producing and consuming nations. For years the United States, as the largest consuming nation, blocked any attempt by the producing nations to fix prices by financing a program to buy surplus production from farmers. This seemingly well-thought-out program was blocked on the grounds that it was anti–free trade and was difficult to finance. After years of trying, some of the member countries, most notably Brazil, took it on themselves to institute their own price support programs independently. For the most part, these programs have worked, but they represent a big risk to scale traders. Should these programs for buying surplus coffee from farmers prove difficult or unpopular for third world governments to finance, they could easily collapse, resulting in a flood of held-back coffee reaching the market all at once. For that reason scale traders should be wary of scaling coffee in years when production is large because that would mean that large amounts of coffee are in hold-back programs with an artificially supported coffee price.

Probably the best source of the statistics you will need for coffee, as well as for sugar and cocoa is, strangely enough, the U.S. Department of Agriculture (USDA). Its Foreign Agricultural Service can be reached at www.fas.usda.gov.

SUGAR

Because sugar is a domestically produced crop, the USDA compiles statistics on this commodity. Much of the U.S. cane sugar is grown in Florida and Louisiana. To support the price of sugar for these growers, the United States imposes a limit on the quantity of sugar that is allowed to be imported into the country. For this reason U.S. cash prices should be ignored entirely. The New York futures contract for #11 sugar is based on world prices.

Sugar cane is grown in tropical and subtropical locations around the world. The two biggest producers are Brazil and India. India's huge population has a sweet tooth. As a result, India is usually a net importer of sugar. Brazil, which produces about the same amount as India, does not have anywhere near the same population, so it is a net exporter, the largest in the world. China is the world's third largest producer and, like India, often imports more than it produces because of its huge population. The next two largest producers are Thailand and Cuba, both of which are big exporters because of their relatively small populations.

Clearly, sugar traders should monitor weather around the world but especially in those major growing areas. To complicate things further, beet sugar, which is grown in far northern areas, such as Idaho in the United States, is also deliverable against the New York and London sugar contracts. In Europe, Russia is a big beet sugar producer, but it does not come close to satisfying its domestic demand; so Russia is also a big importer, especially from its former ally Cuba.

This is a lot to follow, but there is a lot of help, especially at the USDA. To follow sugar fundamentals, probably the best thing to do is to read the USDA's monthly reports and plug the numbers into your balance sheet to come up with your stocks-to-use ratio. Generally, you would like to scale sugar if the price is well below 10 cents a pound and the stocks-to-use ratio is declining. If you do not have sufficient information to know whether the stocks-to-use ratio is declining, I suggest you use a rough rule of thumb that 20 percent or less is an indication that prices are likely too low and supplies are tightening.

COTTON

This is another hot-weather crop. In the United States cotton is grown from Georgia across the southern tier of states into east Texas and also in Arizona and California. California cotton is among the best-quality cotton in the world. Cotton is also grown in Latin America and Asia. Cotton exporters include a variety of nations such as Kazahkstan, Pakistan, and Australia. China also produces a lot of cotton and swings back and forth from being an importer to an exporter, depending on its crop size and domestic usage.

Cotton prices in the United States are affected most by world prices, but they are also subject to government programs, such as the Step II export subsidy program. This program is inconsistently applied according to the current politics of Congress, as it must be voted on each year.

In general, I would ignore the Step II program in my analysis and focus instead on the world supply-and-demand situation. If Congress approves a Step II program, that does raise prices, at least temporarily; but prices only come down once the subsidies are used up. In the end the world market will only pay so much for whatever the supply-and-demand situation is, and that is what we are trying to figure out. In my opinion, focusing on any government subsidy programs will only complicate, unnecessarily, the fundamental picture that a scale trader is trying to develop.

Because cotton is such an important U.S. crop, the USDA gives a very complete report that includes supply-and-demand figures for the United States and for the world. Once again, you should try to obtain a stocks-to-use ratio and find the trend in that number. In general, if it is at 20 percent or lower and prices are low, you have a good scale candidate.

When scale trading cotton, it is a good idea to keep an eye on the world economic situation. Cotton is used primarily for clothing fiber. When there are economic problems, people tend to put off buying new clothes. This is especially true in third world countries where cotton is very popular for clothing.

Crude oil prices also should be monitored. If crude oil prices get very low—below $14 per barrel—the cost of synthetic fiber gets very competitive and starts to take business away from cotton.

10

USING SEASONAL INFORMATION THE RIGHT WAY

The proliferation of seasonal information on commodities has become quite popular in recent years. Understanding its popularity is not hard. Steve Moore's seasonal research, produced by the Moore Research Center, is so widely used that the Chicago Mercantile Exchange has sent out his work on livestock seasonals for free. When you look at this information, you begin to see why it's so popular. Typically, you will find something like this: "In the past 10 years, if you had bought crude oil on February 2 and held it until April 22, you would have made money every year." Sounds like a sure thing, doesn't it? Example after example is presented. Traders buy the books and the research, follow the dates very carefully . . . and lose money. What? That's right, they lose money. Why?

SEASONAL TENDENCIES

The truth is that trades that have worked every year for the past 10 years may have no better than a 50 percent chance of working in the 11th year. This is because of two things about seasonals: First, many so-called seasonals are not really seasonals at all but just statistical anomalies. The amount of price data in commodities is so huge that you are bound to come up with some incidences in which the same direction occurred in a market at the same approximate time of year for many years. Remember, commodities can only go up, down, or sideways. Some of the so-called seasonals that you read about are nothing more than coincidences.

Second, other seasonals that have very real reasons for occurring based on product cycles of supply or demand may not perform in any given year. For instance, when farmers harvest corn in the fall, it creates a temporary oversupply of corn because most of the corn for the year comes to market at one time. Seasonally, therefore, you can expect a decline in corn prices in the fall. The problem is it doesn't happen every year. Some years there is a frost that damages the corn before it is mature and sends prices higher rather than lower in the fall. Also, even though prices decline most years, they do not decline at the same time every year.

I agree wholeheartedly with the use of seasonal tendencies. But I feel that blindly trading seasonals on a calendar-date basis just because it worked that way in the past is not a good way to try to make a living.

With the spread of computers, the ability of people to uncover seasonal patterns has grown tremendously. To make use of this information, you will need to understand what it is that drives the seasonal pattern. The fact that gold prices went up between x and y dates for the past 15 years tells us very little. What it does tell us is that as long as this is not a statistical anomaly, there may be a good reason for gold to go up during that period. If we know the reason, we may be able to determine whether that reason exists this year. Once you understand why gold went up between those dates, you can check to see what's happening this year. Is it likely to repeat this year, or will extenuating circumstances change the picture this year? This is very important.

The only way I know to tell the difference between a real seasonal tendency and a statistical anomaly is to find out what the fundamental basis is behind the move. Furthermore, knowing the fundamental factors behind a seasonal move is the only way for you to get a real clue as to whether you can expect the same move to occur this year.

Let me give you a real-life example. There is a seasonal tendency for December heating oil to be stronger in price than December unleaded gas from mid-August through mid-October. There's no surprise in this, and it is easy to understand why the fundamentals would favor this spread at that time of year. Jobbers are laying in supplies of heating oil for the coming winter while demand for unleaded gas from the summer-driving-season is on the decline. But the spread, which worked very well year after year for 10 years, did not work in 1992. Why? Because in the fall of 1992 there was a shortage of unleaded gas.

It is important to know why a seasonal pattern exists from a fundamental point of view. Once you know that, you can investigate whether the usual seasonal fundamental conditions exist this year so that you don't get caught as all the seasonal energy traders did in 1992.

USING SEASONAL CHARTS

Knowledge of seasonal tendencies coupled with good fundamental analysis can be extremely useful to the scale trader. One of the best places to start your seasonal research is to get someone else to do the computer crunching for you. Steve Moore of Moore Research has done a very good job with this. His annual publication *Seasonal Pattern Charts* is one of the most dog-eared books in our office.

An experienced trader showed me the best way to use these charts. Look at Figure 10.1, a seasonal chart for December wheat futures. The solid line on this chart represents the average price movement for December wheat over the past 15 years. The dotted line represents the average price movement over the past 5 years. The trader pointed out that what you want to look for is patterns where the 5-year and 15-year lines match each other. The importance of this is that it shows that the pattern is most likely still relevant and that the market conditions that produced the long-term pattern have not changed significantly. For instance, you can see that both lines show a tendency for price to decline into the summer and then advance into the fall.

Once you have identified a consistent pattern on the chart, you need to identify the fundamental logic, if there is any, behind this pattern. In the case of wheat, the reasons for the pattern are easy to understand because 75 percent of the wheat grown in the United States is winter wheat. Winter wheat is planted in the fall. It germinates and sprouts, then is covered with snow, and goes dormant for the rest of the winter. In late winter or early spring it resumes growing and is ready to harvest by early summer.

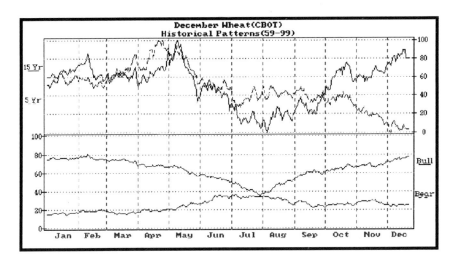

Figure 10.1 December wheat, historical patterns, 1959–1999. (*Source: FutureSource/Bridge*)

The harvest generally begins in June in Texas and continues north through the summer until it is completed in September in Minnesota. Storage facilities exist to store approximately half of this harvest. The rest gets sold immediately. This produces a temporary oversupply, depressing the market until all that wheat can be used or sold abroad. So every year wheat gets depressed during the summer harvest. When the harvest is complete, the selling pressure comes off the market and the price gradually rises all fall until supplies become available from the Southern Hemisphere sometime in December.

Now you have a regular seasonal pattern that can be seen on the charts on a 5-year and a 15-year basis. You understand the fundamentals that produce this pattern. So if the price is approaching the bottom third of the historical trading range for wheat and you are in the May, June, or July time period, you know that you probably have a really good scale candidate. You are probably approaching the lows for the year. The combination of approaching historical low-price territory at the right seasonal time frame can be very powerful.

You only need to know one thing: What are the fundamentals this year? Do they support the idea that the normal seasonal pattern will be followed? Is the approximate low price predicted by the fundamentals within our budget? If you can answer these questions in the affirmative, then it's time to begin your scale. This use of seasonals can be very powerful for the scale trader.

PART III

SCALE TRADING IN ACTION

In this section, we discuss the process of building a scale trade: entering the market and taking profits and such practical considerations as dealing with contract rollovers and selecting a broker.

11

HOW TO CONSTRUCT
A SCALE

Now, we get down to the nuts and bolts of scale trading. I'll use several market examples to illustrate the process of building a scale position.

Constructing a scale trade is not particularly difficult, but it can be tedious. Therefore, I recommend the use of a computer. Not only does a computer make the process easier and faster, but it also makes it possible to try many different types of scales to see how they look. This is important because it enables you to try lots of different "what if" scenarios. It is through the trial and error of looking at many different scales that you can best determine which scales will work best for you, considering your capital, your overall portfolio, and the volatility of the market you wish to scale. But, computer or no, you must first learn the proper mechanics for building a scale position.

SOYBEAN OIL SCALE

Let's look at a truly classic scale, soybean oil. Figure 11.1 shows 23 years of monthly soybean oil prices. First, take a look at the general range of bean oil. Over the past 20 years the price of bean oil has generally ranged from 16 cents to 30 cents a pound, with a low of 13 cents in 1986 and a high of 41 cents in 1984. This general range gives us a basis for a bean oil scale, useable only in some years when prices are in the bottom third of the historical price range. The bottom third in this case is from 16 cents to about 21 cents. Using that

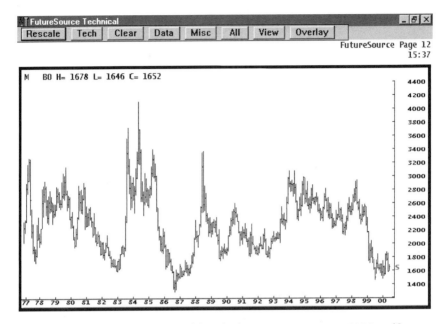

Figure 11.1 Soybean oil, historical patterns, 1977–2000. (*Source:* FutureSource/Bridge)

range, we can construct a sample scale for bean oil beginning at 21 cents down to 15 cents. I'm assuming that you have checked the fundamentals and are confident that prices are now low enough on a fundamental basis.

In Chapter 1, I mentioned that scale trading involved buying on a scale-down basis and setting a discreet sell objective for each contract you buy. Take a look at the bean oil scale in Figure 11.2 for an example of a scale in action. The scale increment is 1 cent; 1 cent in bean oil is worth $600. If you used the sample scale in this example, you would start buying contracts at 21 cents a pound and then buy another contract at each 1 cent lower—20 cents, 19 cents, 18 cents, . . . , down to 15 cents. Remember the discussion in Chapter 1— each time you buy, you set a sell order. If you had bought at 21 cents, you immediately set a good-'til-canceled sell order at 22 cents. When you buy at 20 cents, you immediately set a good-'til-canceled sell order at 21 cents, and so on.

Commodity: Soybean oil
Maintenance margin: $700
Starting price: 21¢
Buy-down increment: 1¢
Profit/loss per cent: $600
Total buy levels: 7
Contracts at each level: 1

	1	2	3	4	5	6	7	8
					Cumulative . . .			
Buy Level	Buy Price (cents/lb.)	No. of Contracts Held	Losing Contracts	Lose per Contract	Loss per Contract	Loss on All Contracts	Required Margin	Minimum Account Funds
1	21	1	0	$ 0	$ 0	$ 0	$ 700	$ 700
2	20	2	1	600	600	600	1,400	2,000
3	19	3	2	600	1,200	1,800	2,100	3,900
4	18	4	3	600	1,800	3,600	2,800	6,400
5	17	5	4	600	2,400	6,000	3,500	9,500
6	16	6	5	600	3,000	9,000	4,200	13,200
7	15	7	6	600	3,600	12,600	4,900	17,500

Figure 11.2 Soybean oil scale.

Now let's go back and look at the charts from several years. If you look at the December 1992 contract (Figure 11.3), for instance, you can see that you could have had a number of buys and sells. As the range oscillated between 20 cents and 22 cents for the first half of the year, you would have been able to follow the plan just discussed by buying at 21 cents and 20 cents, taking profits at 21 cents on your buy at 20 cents and at 22 cents on your buy at 21 cents and then doing it again, buying each time it declined and taking profits each time it moved higher. Eventually, you would have extended your buys to 21, 20, and 19 cents, with sells at 20 and 21 cents.

In 1993 (Figure 11.4) you would have had similar opportunities in the first half of the year, buying at 21 cents and selling at 22 cents. In 1994 and 1995, with higher prices (Figure 11.5 and Figure 11.6), we would not have scaled soybean oil because prices were above the bottom third of the historical price range for bean oil. Recall, as we discussed in Chapter 2, that we focus our scale trade activities only on the bottom third of the historical price range for a commodity.

Figure 11.2 provides a sample of a typical scale model that my company provides for our clients. Column 1 represents each price at

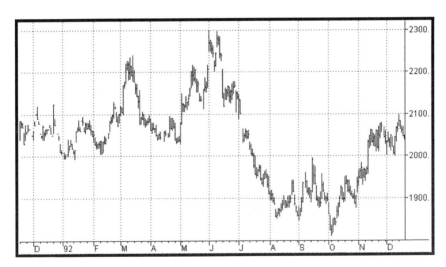

Figure 11.3   December 1992 soy oil futures. (*Source:* OmegaResearch)

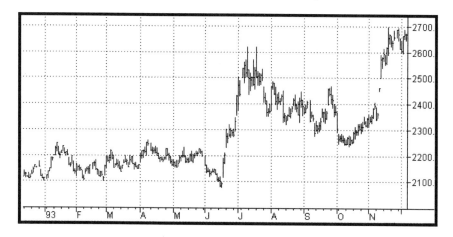

Figure 11.4 December 1993 soy oil futures. (*Source:* OmegaResearch)

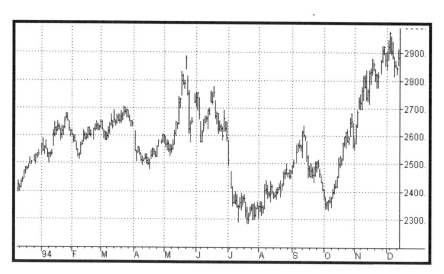

Figure 11.5 December 1994 soy oil futures. (*Source:* OmegaResearch)

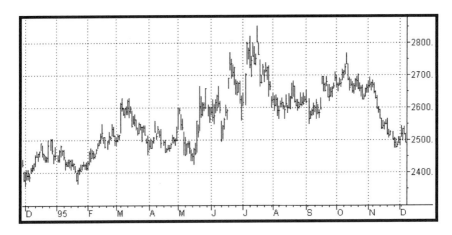

Figure 11.6 December 1995 soy oil futures. (*Source:* OmegaResearch)

which a new buy will be executed. A uniform number of contracts is purchased at each increment. If you are buying one contract at a time, then you would buy one at 21 cents, one at 20 cents, one at 19 cents, and so on. If you are going to buy two at a time, then you would buy two at 21 cents, two at 20 cents, and so on. The scale shown is for a one-contract scale.

Column 2 simply represents the number of contracts owned at each price. At 21 cents you own one, at 20 cents you own two, at 19 cents you own three.

Column 3 represents the number of contracts being held at a loss; this number is always one unit less than the number in column 2.

Column 4 is the amount lost on a single contract since the last purchase. This number is important because, as we shall see, you do not always buy at the same price interval all the way down.

Column 5 is the number in column 3 multiplied by the number in column 4. This gives you the total losses on all the contracts you are carrying since the last purchase was made.

Column 6 is a little tricky. The number in column 6 is the total accumulated losses of all contracts in your inventory since you started buying. Row 1 is your first purchase; this will always be zero because you have no losses yet. The column 6 number in row 2, when you bought your second contract, represents the loss on one contract since your last purchase; for this scale that is $600. Beginning with row 3, you can obtain the figure for column 6 simply by adding the number in column 5 to the number in column 6 in the row immediately above the one where you are now. For row 3 this means adding the number from row 3, column 5 ($1,200) to the number from row 2, column 6 ($600). So the number for row 3, column 6 is $1,200 + $600, or $1,800. For row 4, add the number from row 4, column 5 to the number from row 3, column 6 ($1,800 + $1,800 = $3,600); and so on.

I know this sounds complicated, but it really isn't. Column 6 represents the total losses to date, while column 5 represents the total losses since the last purchase. By adding the total losses at the *time* of your last purchase with the total losses *since* your last purchase, you get the number you are seeking.

Column 7 represents the margin required for each contract you hold. In this example, the margin for soybean oil is $700 (margins fluctuate so when you construct scales, be sure to check with your broker to get the current rate). You take $700, or whatever the margin is for the scale you are constructing, and multiply it by the number of contracts.

Column 8 is the sum of columns 6 and 7. This figure represents the total capital required in your account at each price level.

Once you have constructed your scale, you can quickly look at the bottom row in column 8 to know how much money it will take to trade this scale. In the bean oil example, this figure is $17,500. It is very important to understand that this is only a starting place to estimate how much capital you will need. Nothing at all says that because you or your advisers believe that the price of a commodity won't go below a certain level that, in fact, it won't. In reality you will find that prices occasionally drop below the lowest price for which you had planned. Therefore, you must be prepared to have more capital than the figure given in column 8. As a rule of thumb, I would use 20 percent to 30 percent more capital than the figure in column 8. The critical thing here is that you do not want to place yourself in the situation of running out of money before prices start to rise.

PLATINUM SCALE

Before moving on, let's look at another market and review the process. In this example we will set up a scale for platinum, which has been a very scalable market for years. *(Author's note: At the time this book was revised in early 2000, platinum had rallied to very high prices, above $500 an ounce, and was no longer in scaleable range. I left this discussion in anyway because it is a very good illustration of the kind of process you should go through in setting up a scale.)*

Before actually scaling platinum, you should check to see if the same general fundamentals still apply. But here is why I liked it as this book was being written. As noted in Chapter 7, there are only three platinum mines of any size in the world, two of which are in South Africa. These two mines are very efficient, but they do have a problem. The miners are almost exclusively black, and the managers are white. Because the white managers make a lot more money than the miners do, there are strikes once or twice per year. Every time there is a strike, the price of platinum jumps, often providing us with an opportunity to sell some or all of any platinum contracts into which we might have previously scaled.

The third platinum mine is in Siberia and is every bit in tune with the new Russia—it doesn't work. The Siberian mine is thought to have approximately 25 percent of the world's platinum supply. Under the Soviets there were centralized industries, and the high-powered drills necessary for platinum mining were manufactured at a factory in Azerbijan. That factory was destroyed in the civil war there. As of the writing of this book, the Russians are not known to have imported any of these rather expensive drills.

Through most of the 1990s the Russians were big sellers of precious metals. It is one of the few ways they had of getting hard currency. Prior to the 1990s the Russians had built up very large aboveground stockpiles for strategic purposes. Once they started shipping platinum supplies, prices dropped; but, more important for the current time, the constant shipments masked the production problems they were having. The last of these shipments arrived in Switzerland in 1996 and 1997 in boxes marked with the Red Army insignia on it. This was the last of their aboveground supply. Russia did not ship any platinum from January through July 1997 and from January through October 1998, and shipments have continued to be sporadic since then.

Now keep the Russian situation in mind for a moment, and look at the breakdown of where the world gets its platinum. South Africa has been increasing its market share steadily and is up to more than 70 percent of world production. Russia is down to only about a 15 percent market share. The remaining 15 percent comes out of the ground as a by-product of nickel and gold mining. Due to shrinking Russian shipments, world platinum production declined in 1998. Demand, meanwhile, is soaring. The result is that we moved from a very small production surplus in 1996 to a large deficit in production in 1999. In 1996 the world produced 8,000 ounces of surplus platinum. In a world that consumed about 6 million ounces of platinum, 8,000 ounces is less than one day's supply. The supply/demand balance fell to a deficit of 30,000 ounces in 1997, a deficit of some 50,000 ounces in 1998, and 730,000 ounces in 1999.

Now look at the monthly platinum chart (Figure 11.7). Prices generally declined from mid-1997 through much of 1999 to approximately the same prices that existed when the Russians were dumping their aboveground stockpiles. How could this be? The answer lies in Japan. Japan bought about 39 percent of the world's platinum in 1999, down from 45 percent the previous year. While total world platinum demand is growing, Japan's demand, still the largest by far, shrank and the price declined. Although this could go on, the continued increase in demand worldwide, leading to increasing production deficits, means that eventually the decline in Japan's demand will

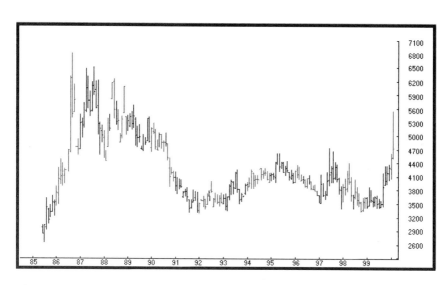

Figure 11.7 Platinum, historical pattern, 1985–1999. (*Source:* FutureSource/Bridge)

RECOMMENDED SCALE TRADE PLAN

Commodity	
Month	
Starting price	
Maintenance margin	
Profit/loss per $	
Buy-down increment	
Sell-profit increment	
Total buy levels	
Contracts at each level	

PLEASE REMEMBER THAT COMMODITY TRADING IN-
VOLVES A HIGH DEGREE OF LEVERAGE. THAT LEVERAGE
ALLOWS FOR LARGE RETURNS BUT ALSO LARGE LOSSES.
DUE TO THE HIGH DEGREE OF RISK INVOLVED IN HIGH
LEVERAGE, YOU SHOULD CAREFULLY CONSIDER
WHETHER COMMODITY TRADING IS APPROPRIATE FOR
YOU. AS ALWAYS, MARKET CONDITIONS MAY MAKE IT
DIFFICULT, IF NOT IMPOSSIBLE, TO EXECUTE ORDERS.

	1		2	3	4	5	6	7	8
Buy Level	Buy Price	Sell Price	No. of Contracts Held	Losing Contracts	Loss per Contract	Possible Cumulative Loss per Contract	Possible Cumulative Loss on All Contracts	Cumulative Required Margin	Minimum Account Funds
1									
2									
3									
4									
5									
6									
7									

Figure 11.8 Platinum scale.

have little or no effect on the price. Those deficits are very likely to send the price soaring. Meanwhile, we had a scale trader's dream because we had shrinking production (thanks to the Russians), increasing demand, and a declining price.

Let's see how we could construct a scale to take advantage of this. Looking back at the price history (Figure 11.7), you can see that from 1991 through 1999 the price of platinum traded between $470 and $330 an ounce, making the bottom third of the range $376 to $330. Because you can't guess when the price will stop declining, even though you might believe it could be soon, you may want to be a little conservative in picking the bottom third of the range. You might ignore the spike highs of 1995 and 1997 and focus on the range from $430 to $330. This makes the bottom third $363 down to $330; and because $363 is an odd number, you might further reduce your top buy to $360.

Now fill in the columns on your worksheet (Figure 11.8). Let's see what it looks like if you buy every $5 down in platinum. That will give you seven contracts if the price declines all the way to $330. So you can write in $360, $355, $350, . . . , down to $330 in column 1. Now just go back to the description earlier in this chapter of how to build a scale grid, and fill it in for platinum. It should look like Figure 11.8.

COMPUTERIZING YOUR SCALE

So now you know how to construct a scale. The true students among you should stop reading, get a paper and pencil, and start constructing a few hypothetical scales. If you don't know the margin for a particular market, don't worry. Just make it up. You're only practicing now. Those of you who are settled down on the couch reading this book like a novel should really get up now and try this exercise. Don't worry about me, I'll just turn on the TV while you're gone.

You're back? Good. Well, now you know something else: It's tedious work constructing those scales, isn't it? There's got to be a better way, you must be thinking. There is . . . with a computer. And, luckily, you don't need to pay thousands of dollars for a specialized piece of trading software. All you need is a spreadsheet program such as Excel. Appendix III explains how to use the Excel spreadsheet on the disk in the back of this book to make your own scales.

There is a tremendous advantage to doing scales on the computer. Doing it by hand is so tedious that you tend to basically guess about what the right scale might be; then once you have worked it out, you're not very motivated to experiment with other possibilities. A computer spreadsheet allows you to try a variety of scale possibilities easily and quickly. This makes it easy to see, for example, what the difference might be between scaling corn every 2 cents versus every 3 cents.

FINE-TUNING YOUR SCALE

Although some tweaking may be necessary, it is not advisable to fine-tune your scale too much. Because you do not know what the actual low of the market will be, you will always be guessing about how much capital you will actually need. Setting up a scale in the manner outlined in the previous sections gives you a plan. If your spreadsheet suggests you need $16,000, you have a starting point; but be prepared to supply additional funds as described earlier. In the end you may have needed anything from $1,000 to $20,000 or more.

Certain elements of your scale position can be adjusted, depending on market conditions and your trading goals.

Buy Intervals

It is not necessary to scale in each of your buys at the same interval. In our soybean oil scale, for example, we bought at 100-point intervals. We could have started the scale buying every 100 points lower and then changed to every 50 points lower as the price dropped below 19 cents. This would require more capital, but with our computerized spreadsheet we can quickly determine how much more money we would need. The point here is that there are many ways to lay out your buys.

There are two reasons why you might want to increase the frequency of your buys as price decreases. First, you want to keep your scale trading intervals constant on a percentage basis rather than a point basis. At lower prices, a particular price move of, say, 10 points is bigger on a percentage basis than the same move at higher price levels. For example, when the price is 2500, a 2 percent move is 50 points;

when the price is at 1900, a 2 percent move is 38 points (even with volatility remaining constant). So, in absolute point terms, price moves tend to be smaller as the price declines.

Second, as price declines, percentage volatility tends to decline as well. This is because price declines tend to be characterized by a loss of interest in the market. Typically, fewer and fewer participants are involved as the market continues to drop. Eventually, people lose all interest in the market, and price action becomes almost lifeless. If your scale is to buy at constant intervals of 100 points, you may find you are getting less frequent buys as the market moves lower. This may not be the best thing for your plans. You need to buy because unless you acquire inventory while prices are falling, you will have nothing to profit from when prices rise.

At the risk of complicating things here, there may be situations when you would actually want to do the opposite—you might, under certain situations, buy less frequently as prices decline. This will probably come about as a reaction to a relentless price drop or because you incorrectly gauged how low the market could go. Under such circumstances it may be advisable to spread your buys out a little as the market approaches its bottom. As a matter of self-preservation, it may be necessary either to cease buying altogether or to buy less frequently. I prefer to buy less frequently if possible; "why" will become evident in the next chapter in our discussion of when to take profits.

Other Modifications

Here's another way to modify a scale. Suppose you are considering trading a commodity that is unlikely to drop very low this year. Because of the promising fundamental situation, you are tempted to begin scaling at a higher price than would normally be called for by the study of a long-term chart. You could do this by using a wider interval between buys. But it also can be done by starting with smaller contracts on the MidAmerica Commodity Exchange (Mid-Am) at the higher prices and then changing to full-size contracts at lower prices. This approach has the advantage of keeping capital requirements reasonable, allowing you to begin buying at a higher price level than you otherwise would without forcing you into using too wide a scale.

The MidAm is a small exchange that is part of the Chicago Board of Trade (CBOT). It specializes in trading contracts identical to the contracts traded on many other commodity exchanges, except that they are smaller. For example, the size of the live cattle contract of the Chicago Mercantile Exchange (CME) is 40,000 pounds; the MidAm live cattle contract is identical to the CME contract except that it is only 20,000 pounds. MidAm contracts are often referred to as "minis."

Let's say you wanted to scale cattle, but you have a problem. Prices were a little high from a historical perspective, but the fundamentals this year pointed to still higher prices overall. So you'd like to begin scaling at a higher-than-usual price. You could do this by spreading out your buys so you would still have the same number of contracts as usual at the lowest prices in your scale. This would result in a higher capital requirement, but probably not excessively higher. The problem is that if your buys are too far apart, you may miss out on oscillation trades.

Oscillation Trades

These trades, which result from prices trading in a narrow range, are often the best part of scale trading. Narrow-range trading usually drives traders nuts. Every time the market goes up, they buy, expecting higher prices, only to be disappointed. Every time the market declines, they sell, looking for lower prices, only to see the market rise right back up to the top of the range, probably stopping them out with a loss. These are the situations in which scale trading really shines.

When everyone else is selling, the scale trader is buying. Then, when the market is going up and everyone else is reversing their positions, taking losses on their shorts and going long, the scale trader is taking profits on his long position and waiting for another opportunity to buy. Price goes up and down, with the scale trader racking up profits while others are getting chewed up with losses.

If your scale is too wide, you run the risk of missing out on the fun and the profit of oscillation trades in sideways markets. Instead of having a wide scale to start buying higher, you can start buying at a higher level with MidAm contracts. This way you can keep a reasonably narrow range between your buys, have a better chance of capitalizing on oscillation trades, and not increase your capital requirements drastically.

STOPS REVISITED

A question often arises when I describe scale trading: What about stops? We discussed this topic briefly in Chapter 3, but there is more to be said on this subject. First, we don't use stops in scale trading. This statement often sends panic into the hearts of commodity traders. Every other book you have ever read has probably beaten the necessity of stops into your brain: "Never place an order without also placing a stop," "Don't use mental stops," and so on. All sorts of hard-and-fast rules have been pounded into you over and over again.

There are many good reasons why this is hammered on so much. The most important reason is that your plan of exiting a trade is probably more important than your plan for entering a trade. Getting into a trade is easy. Getting out is a much harder decision. You need to have a plan for realizing your profits and also a plan for what to do when you are wrong.

Getting into a trade at the right price and time is important, but not knowing when to get out can cost you dearly. If you've ever watched a $500 or $1,000 profit turn into a loss, you know what I'm talking about. Without a good exit plan, profits often turn into losses, and small losses have a tendency to grow into a catastrophic loss. Scale trading uses a very well-defined exit plan, which we will discuss in Chapter 12. The fear most traders have about not using stops in scale trading is that prices will go down forever and eat their account whole. This is a legitimate fear, but stops don't necessarily solve the problem. They may only make it worse.

Consider this: How many trades have you been stopped out of with a loss, trades that would have resulted in a profit if your stop had not been hit? Is the problem your stop placement? Perhaps. I am not advocating abolishing stops here. What I am getting at is that sometimes it might be better to not use stops than to use them. One of those times is in scale trading.

A little discussion will help to alleviate the fears of those traders who have been indoctrinated on the use of stops. First, remember there is a limit to how low prices can go. A commodity can never be valueless, can never drop to a negative price. This is why we only scale trade from the long side—although prices may be able to go up forever, they cannot go down forever.

Second, commodities also have practical price floors built into them by the cost of production. Yes, prices can and do drop below cost of production but usually not for long or by much because producers get forced out of business by losses. Once we have identified those practical floors, we can protect ourselves by never beginning to scale very high above them. The ideal—what we are really trying to do—is buy the low. The ideal scale would consist of only one buy. Because consistent bottom-picking is almost impossible, we must have a plan to deal with being wrong. Our plan is to buy more.

BUYING INVENTORY

This is where we run into another case of scale trading flying in the face of everything you have ever been told about commodity trading. "Don't add to losers," you've been told. Under most circumstances, this is good advice. But scale trading is unlike most other trading. A better way to look at scale trading is to forget that you are trading commodity futures.

Think of yourself simply as being in the business of buying things that you will mark up for sale at a later date. When you are buying, you are acquiring inventory. That inventory will have certain costs associated with it—storage, insurance, interest, and so on. If you can acquire more inventory at cheaper prices and pass the savings on to your customers, you can make more sales. The same concept holds true for scale trading. You are looking to buy cheap, starting with your first purchase. If you can buy more inventory at lower prices, you are eager to do so because it means you will be able to make more sales.

There are certain costs associated with carrying your inventory, such as margin, paper losses on your inventory, and commissions. You can expect that when you are in the inventory-gathering stage, you will see the value of your account decline by 30 percent or more. However, you are acquiring an inventory of a commodity that will probably always be in demand (under what circumstances would people not want to buy wheat?). If you buy wisely (that is, cheaply enough), you should never have to put your inventory on sale at a discount and take a loss.

The key is to know your business. The careful study of fundamentals, seasonals, and charts will put you in position to know the right time to buy. If you were in the hat business, you would know you have to buy straw hats in January that you will sell in the summertime.

When Bernard Baruch, the famous 1930s stock investor, was asked how he made so much money, he responded, "Simple. I buy my straw hats in January." Another time he answered the same question by saying, "I try to be accommodating. When everyone wants to sell, I buy. When everyone wants to buy, I sell." This is the gist of scale trading: systematic contrarian trading.

12

TAKING PROFITS

This is the fun part. If you've done everything right up to now, you are holding an inventory of contracts, most at a loss. What happens next? Sooner or later (hopefully sooner) the laws of economics prevail, and the price will start to rise naturally. As you remember from Chapter 1, this is because when prices get low enough to be unprofitable for producers, they are forced to curtail production at the very time that the low price is stimulating demand. Once these economic forces take over, there is no place for the price to go but up.

PLAN YOUR SELLS

Now is the time to execute the second part of your plan—selling your inventory at a profit. The way you want to do this is to decide how much profit you think you can get per contract and then sell each contract at that marked-up value.

For instance, suppose you have been buying soybean oil at 100-point (one-cent) intervals—21 cents, 20 cents, and 19 cents. Now the price starts to rise. You have determined that, given current market conditions, you can expect to achieve a profit of 100 points per contract, which is equal to $600 in bean oil. What you want to do is to offer the contract you bought at 19 cents for sale at 20 cents. Once that is sold, you will be looking to sell your 20-cent contract at 21 cents, and then your 21-cent contract at 22 cents.

Now let's look at Figure 12.1. It is the same bean oil scale we constructed in Chapter 11 (Figure 11.2) but with additional sell information and with record-keeping spaces inserted.

Commodity: Soybean oil
Maintenance margin: $700
Starting price: 21¢
Buy-down increment: 1¢
Profit/loss per cent: $600
Total buy levels: 7
Contracts at each level: 1

	1				2	3	4	5	6	7	8
								Cumulative . . .			
Buy Level	Buy Price (cents/lb.)	Date Order Placed	Date Order Filled	Sell Price (cents/lb.)	No. of Contracts Held	Losing Contracts	Loss per Contract	Loss per Contract	Loss on All Contracts	Required Margin	Minimum Account Funds
1	21			22	1	0	$ 0	$ 0	$ 0	$ 700	$ 700
2	20			21	2	1	600	600	600	1,400	2,000
3	19			20	3	2	600	1,200	1,800	2,100	3,900
4	18			19	4	3	600	1,800	3,600	2,800	6,400
5	17			18	5	4	600	2,400	6,000	3,500	9,500
6	16			17	6	5	600	3,000	9,000	4,200	13,200
7	15			16	7	6	600	3,600	12,600	4,900	17,500

Figure 12.1 Bean oil scale worksheet.

It is very important that you plan your sells in this manner. Many people make the mistake of confusing scale trading with the stock investor's technique of averaging down. This technique is simple. If you bought a stock at $40 and again at $36 and again at $32, you figure out your average—in this case, $36—and try to sell all your stock at one time at your average price plus your desired profit. Averaging down is not scale trading, and the scale trader potentially would be making a very costly mistake to plan his sells in this manner.

The reason why this is a mistake has to do with oscillations, which we discussed in Chapter 11. It is very unusual for markets to drop straight down, stop declining, and immediately go straight up. It does happen occasionally, and our plan does accommodate that situation. But our plan will really excel at the situation that normally prevails—the market goes down and up in stages or oscillations.

Using our soybean oil sample scale again, perhaps the market drops to 20.95 cents on the day. We have an order to buy at 21 cents, which is executed. We now have one contract. The next day maybe the low is 20.80 and the high is 21.30. We are still holding the one contract we bought at 21 cents. The day after that the low is 21.05 and the high is 21.55, and we are still holding that one contract. The market then goes down for three days, each day having a lower high and a lower low than the previous day. Prices have now declined to 19.75 cents. Prices have not yet advanced enough to sell the one contract we bought at 21 cents. If we are using the bean oil scale example from Chapter 11, we will have bought a second contract on the way down at 20 cents. The next week the market rallies to 21.35 cents before resuming its decline.

Now, if we had been averaging down, we would have figured our average price at 20.50 cents. If we wanted to make an average of 100 points per contract, we would need to get a price of 21.50 before we would sell. The scale trader would have sold at 21 cents and then bought again at 20 cents on the way down. The averager would still be holding two contracts, never having taken a profit on either one. If the market spent the next two weeks going back and forth from 19.75 to 21.35 cents, the scale trader would cash in one winner after the other while the averager sat there waiting for a price that never came.

Continuing with our hypothetical situation, suppose that after two weeks of going sideways between 19.75 and 21.35 cents, the market then dropped pretty steadily down to 16.75. After doing that, the market rallied to 18.75 and dropped again back to 16.75 cents. The averager is again sitting and waiting for a price that does not come while the scale trader gets another profitable trade. Because markets spend a considerable amount of time going sideways and generally being choppy, the scale trader will be able to realize superior profits over the trader who is averaging down.

In the market that goes straight down and then straight up, both traders will realize the same profit. It is true that the averager will come out ahead of the scale trader if the scale trader has an inventory of contracts bought at prices that are just too high. The averager may be able to get all his contracts sold at a profit while the scale trader is still carrying those high-priced contracts waiting for a profit.

Often, however, the scale trader will still be ahead due to the oscillation profits. While it's true that there are a few situations when the averager will come out ahead, my opinion is that it is not worth considering as an appropriate strategy. Stick with what will work best in most of the different imaginable situations.

PLAN YOUR PROFIT

Having settled that (I hope), we need to address a difficult problem. How do you know how much profit to expect? Mostly, it's a guess. But you can make it an educated guess. How much profit you can expect is a function of market volatility. This is a place where the old saying "Bulls make money, bears make money, and pigs get slaughtered" comes to mind.

Many traders are of the mind-set that they want to hit home runs. If a trade doesn't have the potential to make thousands of dollars, why do it? They take loss after loss, looking for the elusive monster trade. If they are either wealthy, patient, or lucky, they will eventually find it. But it's so much easier and saner to accept modest profits that have the chance to be realized on almost every trade. For many investors it may be the only way they will ever be profitable.

In deciding how much profit to take on your scales, you need to get a handle on market volatility. If you've been trading for a long time, you may be able to do this by feel. For most people, including long-time traders, it's probably better to take a little measurement first.

Take a moving average of the highs of the past 20 days. Then take a moving average of the lows of the past 20 days. Subtract the average of the lows from the average of the highs. This will give you an average range of the past 20 days, which is a way to measure market volatility. The larger the average range, the greater the volatility;

the smaller the average range, the lower the volatility. To refine this further, you can also do the same calculation for the past 5 days and compare this figure to the 20-day calculation to see if there are any significant changes taking place in market volatility.

This figure will give you a good guide on what you can expect from the market. If you are scaling corn, for instance, you may find that the daily volatility is about 3 cents. As a profit objective, I would not try for more than twice the daily volatility, so you could set your profit goal at 6 cents. Not that you will always do it that way—you might go for only 3 cents. At first many investors balk at taking only $150 per contract in profits. After all, you have to pay commissions out of that. But if the market is trading in a very narrow range, you might wait months to get one 6-cent profit while the trader looking for 3 cents may have cashed in dozens of winning trades.

I have actually had this happen in our brokerage. In 1993 two traders were scaling in the silver market. One trader was trying to get 10 cents profit per trade. In silver every penny is $50 so this is a reasonable goal. He eventually got his profit and came out just fine. At the same time another trader, buying at the same price, was willing to settle for only 4 cents per contract. That's only $200 per contract before commissions. Very few traders would be willing to settle for that. Yet, the trader going for 4 cents made more money than the trader going for 10 cents did. The trader going for 4 cents cashed in 10 winning trades for $2,000 before the trader going for 10 cents was able to get his $500. That's quite a difference, even after commissions and fees.

The moral of the story is not that you should always go for smaller profits, but that you should be aware of the kind of market you are in. If the market is very quiet, it is probably better to go for smaller profits. Otherwise, going for between $400 and $600 per trade would be normal.

One more point about deciding when to take profits: market volatility changes. You don't have to adjust your sells continually, but if you notice a marked change in volatility, you need to adjust for that. The most common change occurs when markets get very depressed. The tendency then is for volatility to get compressed. If you started scaling corn at $2.45 and set your sells for 6 cents per contract, be aware that if the market declines to $2.15, you will have a harder time getting 6 cents on your lower-priced contracts.

You might be much better off reducing the amount of profit per contract if the price drops down to the lower end of your scale. This will give you a better chance of racking up oscillation profits. Markets rarely bottom and rocket right up; they usually bottom over long periods of time in a lifeless fashion.

The scale trader trying to get as much profit on his $2.15 corn contract as he was trying to get on his $2.45 contract may find himself in the same situation as the silver trader trying to get $500 per contract in 1993. You'll likely get it, but you might be more profitable adjusting your sells to a lower profit at lower prices.

One more point: Over the years I have found that novice scale traders occasionally, and incorrectly, relate the size of the buying intervals to the size of the profit objective. The incorrect assumption is that if I am scaling down every 100 points, for instance, then my sell objective should be 100 points. This is an incorrect assumption. The fact that occasionally some scales may use the same size buying interval and profit objective is a coincidence. The distance between buys is a consideration related to the size of your capital, the size of drawdown that is acceptable to you, and how far you now are from a projected possible low. The size of the selling objective, as we have just discussed, is a function of current market volatility in which the scale trader takes an educated guess about what size fluctuation it might be reasonable to see in the market.

13

THE DREADED
CONTRACT ROLLOVERS

This subject seems to be the most difficult for new scale traders to grasp. It is actually a very simple phenomenon. What happens when you have bought a number of contracts on the way down and you run out of time on your contract? Answer: A rollover maneuver.

Rolling over refers to the process of liquidating positions in an expiring contract month and reestablishing them in a farther out contract. For example, if you have bought three November soybean futures contracts and November is now approaching, then a rollover becomes necessary. One day soon you will face something called First Notice Day. This is discussed in Appendix I, "Getting a Handle on Futures." The notice I am referring to is a delivery notice. First Notice Day is the first day on which notice of delivery can be made. If you are long the market (that is, if you are holding contracts that you bought), you can be notified of delivery at any time beginning with First Notice Day.

The old myth about a grain truck pulling up outside your house to dump 5,000 bushels of soybeans on your lawn is nothing more than an old myth. *Delivery* just means you will have ownership of the soybeans somewhere else, probably in Chicago.

It's not a big problem to get delivered on. All you do is turn around and sell the contract immediately—problem solved. Still, you wish to avoid this problem because there are additional expenses involved. You will be charged an extra commission plus storage and interest for the energies, which have First Notice Day after the last trading day. In this situation reselling is more difficult and more expensive.

FIRST NOTICE DAY

You may be curious about why most exchanges have a First Notice Day, after which the contract continues to be traded until last trading day. The procedure is set up to allow a period during which contracts are exchange-traded for the purpose of allowing hedgers to make and take delivery. A big deal is made about putting First Notice Day on the calendar so that speculators who do not want to be involved in the delivery process will know when to get out of their contracts.

When First Notice Day is getting close, a scale trader needs to execute a rollover. What you do is sell all the contracts you are holding in the current contract and buy the same number and type of contracts in a farther out month. For example, if you were holding November soybean futures, you would sell the November contracts and buy January or March soybean contracts. Your scale now exists in the new contract months.

A LITTLE FINE-TUNING

One technique that could improve your long-term profitability is to use spread orders to roll over. When you sell the current month and buy the farther out month (sometimes referred to as the "back" month), you are executing a *spread*. There are many kinds of spreads, but the most common type is the *calendar spread,* in which you buy one month and sell another in the same commodity. Even though you are rolling over your scale positions by closing out positions in one month and entering them in another, the order that is placed is the same order that would be placed if you were entering a spread trade. Because this is a common order, you can do a little something here that can help to improve your profitability.

When you enter an order, you have a choice of taking the market price or specifying the price you would like to get. Taking whatever the market will give you is called a *market order*. Specifying a price uses a *limit order*. When you scale trade, you use limit orders to specify the prices at which you will buy and sell. When you roll over, you can do the same. For reasons discussed later in this chapter, there is almost always a differential between the price of the current month and the prices for the back months. These price differentials, also known as the spread (shorthand for the "spread price"), tend to fluctuate daily. As you approach First Notice Day, the tendency is for the price of the back months to be even higher priced relative to the current month. This is because holders of long positions in the current month, in an effort to avoid delivery, are, like you, rolling over by buying the back months and selling the current month. This tends to depress the price of the current month relative to the back month as the current month absorbs all that selling while the back months absorb a spurt of buying.

The little technique you might try is simply this: Two to four weeks in advance of First Notice Day, get a price quote on the rollover spread you plan to execute. If you have the equipment, you would ideally take a look at the recent price range of the spread. If you do not have the equipment and you are using a full-service broker, ask the broker to take a look at the spread chart and to give you an idea of the recent range of prices. With that information in hand, you take a guess about what a reasonable price might be for the spread. Let's say that the range of prices was between 5 and 9 cents and that the current price is 7 cents. You might try to put in a limit order to get your rollover done at 6 cents. Rolling over this way should make it easier for you to achieve your profits ultimately by lowering your rollover premium (which we will discuss shortly).

Should you decide to try rolling over in this fashion, I recommend that you monitor the spread prices every day or at least every few days to see if the spread is trending away from you. In that case you may not want to wait any longer for the market to come to you, knowing that the normal tendency will be for the spread differential to increase as First Notice Day approaches. As you will see later, that would be a worse situation for you. Before we go there, I would like to examine a couple of other aspects of rolling over.

ADJUST SCALE AND PROFIT OBJECTIVES

Once your rollover has been accomplished, you'll have to make a few adjustments in your scale. First, you will have to cancel all of your good-'til-canceled profit (sell) orders for the contracts you have just sold. Second, you will need to enter sell orders for your new contracts. In our example, you would have sold your three contracts of

November soybeans and bought three contracts of March soybeans. You now need to cancel your good-'til-canceled orders to sell November soybeans at your profit objectives and enter new orders to sell March soybeans at your profit objective.

Because of the usual price differences between contract months in the same commodity, you almost certainly will have new profit objectives when you roll over. Let's say you were planning to sell November soybeans at $5.50, $5.75, and $6.00. When it came time to roll over, you sold all your November soybean contracts at $5.25 and bought three March soybean contracts at $5.50, a difference of 25 cents. To get a profit on this trade ultimately, you need to sell your new March soybean contracts at price levels 25 cents higher than your originally planned sell prices. Your new sell points for March soybeans would be placed at $5.75, $6.00, and $6.25.

In other words, you will need to add or subtract the difference between what you sold your old contracts for and what you bought your new contracts for. If the new contracts were at a higher price, you will need to add the difference to your old sell prices. If they were at a lower price, which is an unusual occurrence, you will need to subtract the difference.

TRANSPARENT LOSS

It is important to understand that when you roll over, usually you will be incurring a loss. This occurs because you will have been carrying an inventory of contracts that you acquired at prices that were higher than the current price at the time that you roll over. At that moment you are clearly in a loss position. When you roll over, those losses are realized, and you will receive a statement from your brokerage that shows you losing money.

The question is: Did you really lose money? I don't mean to speak double-talk here, but the answer is yes and no. "Yes" because up to that point you have unquestionably lost money. Not understanding that and where you go next can be unnerving. Remember, you want to hold contracts at a loss. It is the only way you can acquire an inventory. You start almost every scale by going into a loss position first so that you can acquire inventory, which you hope to liquidate at a profit. "No" because at the time of the rollover you have essentially generated a *transparent loss*. What this means is that you have indeed taken a loss on November soybeans, but it is transparent because you have simultaneously acquired an inventory of March soybeans that you hope to sell at a large enough profit to overcome the previous loss on the November soybeans and thereby make a profit on your overall endeavor.

On some rare occasions, it is actually necessary to roll over again. Suppose you rolled over from November to March soybeans and held March soybeans until almost First Notice Day on the March contracts but have not yet achieved a price you need to be profitable. Then you would roll over again, perhaps to the May or July soybean contract, going through the process again of adjusting your sell orders and carrying your inventory forward in the form of November soybean contracts until you reach your profit objectives.

Executing rollovers is simple. There's really not much to it. There are, however, some related issues.

CARRYING CHARGES

I alluded to this earlier when I spoke of the price differential between contract months in the same commodity. First, the price of the contract we are rolling into is usually higher because of carrying charges. Carrying charges are simple to understand. If you want to buy soybeans from me for November delivery and it is now November, I will incur very little expense in the form of insurance, interest, and so on, until I deliver them to you. But if you want to wait until March to take delivery, my expenses, or carrying charges, will obviously be greater.

For those of you interested in nailing things down in fine detail, the carrying charges are most closely related to interest rates. You can usually determine what the fair carrying charges are by figuring what the interest rates would be for the period involved. This means that in periods of high interest rates, the spread between what you sell your old contracts for and what you buy your new contracts for will normally be wider than in periods of low interest rates.

There are two reasons why you will, on a very few occasions, be able to roll over to a new contract trading at a lower price. First, it may be due to seasonal influences. For example, the price of heating oil is often lower in July than in October. Second, the market may be changing into a bull market. In a bull market there is a tendency for the market to become "backward." This technical term refers to that situation when the near months are trading at a premium to the far months.

Carrying charges are an expense incurred by scale traders. Except in those few instances described in the previous paragraph, there's no way around it. To understand the nature of this expense, you need to understand the relationship between the *cash price*—the actual price of the commodity if you were to buy it and take it home today—and the *futures price.*

Due to carrying charges, futures prices are usually higher than cash prices. If cash prices were to remain constant, the natural tendency for the futures price would be to decline as we moved forward in time as the cost of carry reduces as we get closer to delivery. At the time of delivery the futures price should approximate the cash price. For several technical reasons cash prices and futures prices will still be a little different, but the tendency to be approximately the same is clearly there. The futures price will gravitate toward the cash price as the futures near delivery.

In a world of constant cash prices, the scale trader would lose money constantly because they would repeatedly roll over to farther-out-month contracts that only declined in price. Fortunately for us, cash prices are far from constant.

Still, you need to be aware of the effect of carrying charges because they are one variable that may cause you to occasionally lose money scale trading. Once in a while, maybe once every year or two, you will find yourself in a situation where you have been rolling over repeatedly in the same scale. After doing this a few times, you will find that the selling prices you need to have to achieve a profit are just too high.

In these unusual circumstances, where the carrying charges have mounted up, you may have to take the loss. This will usually happen with just one or two contracts, and the losses on those will be substantial, perhaps $1,000 or $2,000. But keep in mind that the more likely situation will be that you will have made at least that much or more on the other contracts you previously cashed in on that scale. If you follow the advice in this book carefully, the situation described here may never happen to you. But it might, so be aware of it.

ROLL TO LIQUIDITY AND VOLATILITY

Let's take a look at the choice of contracts into which you want to roll over. There are several considerations. The most important are liquidity and volatility. You want to buy a contract month that is far enough in the future to give you a chance to reach your objectives, that is liquid enough to ensure that your orders will get filled, and that is volatile enough to give you a good chance to get oscillation profits. The farther out in the future you go, the less liquidity and volatility you will likely find, so you need to balance your needs here for time against volatility and liquidity.

SEASONAL TENDENCIES

You also would be well advised to pay attention to seasonal tendencies. If you are reaching First Notice Day on June crude oil, you may not want to choose December as the month you want to roll into because crude oil tends to decline seasonally during the months of November and December. If you are scaling December crude oil, you will likely be left with an inventory that you will be forced to roll over again to a distant month trading at a higher price. When considering contract months, try to select one that has a tendency to reach First Notice Day on a high note rather than on a weak one.

AVOIDING ROLLOVERS

A final and the most important point about rollovers: You really would rather not be in the situation where you have to roll over. But if you do, don't worry about it. If you can avoid rollovers, so much the better—you will save on commissions and on carrying charges. You can employ several practices to help avoid rollovers.

1. Scale trade in contract months with plenty of time before delivery. Generally, five to six months is good. You will need to consider each commodity separately. Some commodities have very good liquidity in certain contract months well in advance. For instance, you can find lots of volatility and liquidity in December corn futures as early as January or February. On the other hand, you'd better wait until at least June and probably later before you attempt to use December oats for scale trading.

2. As you get closer to delivery in a contract you are scaling, stop buying that contract month in your scale and start buying a farther out month. You may have to roll some of your contracts, but you may avoid rolling a few.

3. In selecting which contract months to scale, check the seasonal tendencies. Cocoa, for instance, exhibits a tendency to decline from January through June. If you scale July cocoa, which has its First Notice Day in June, you run a greater risk of needing to roll over than if you scale September or December cocoa. You will need to check liquidity for these months in making your selection. You also want to avoid paying very high carrying charges, but generally you will want to avoid scaling a month that tends to decline into First Notice Day.

4. Choose a broker with lots of scale trade experience. He or she can be very important to your success at times like these, helping you to navigate the many nuances involved at rollover time.

Careful planning will help you avoid many rollovers, but they are inevitable. So just do it and don't worry. You should almost always come out profitably.

14

OPTIONS

DRAWDOWNS

If you haven't perceived it yet, there is a major drawback to scale trading. Earlier in the book we discussed the necessity of *drawdowns,* which simply are declines in your account value. If you buy a commodity at progressively lower levels, the contracts you acquired early in this campaign are the ones you bought at higher prices and are now showing a loss. This results in a decline in the value of your account—a drawdown. This works very well to a point because it enables you to acquire the inventory you need to be able to sell later—at a profit, you hope. Unless you have an inventory of contracts, you will not be able to make a return because you will have nothing from which you can profit. The bottom line is that, for scale trading to work, you have to experience drawdowns.

The point at which drawdowns become a problem is the point at which a scale trader experiences a market or a group of markets that have declined to prices much below the lowest point that his or her analysis indicated. It seems like this happens on an average of once per year. Drawdowns may be necessary to succeed at scale trading, but they can become too large. Sometimes scale traders incur drawdowns larger than they have planned for or can afford to finance, and, as a result, they must liquidate their scale trades at terrible losses. So any strategy that could control or minimize drawdowns might not only improve your ability to survive those trying times when the drawdowns get large but might also help to smooth out your overall equity curve.

The main concerns when considering such a strategy are:

1. Will the strategy reduce expected returns from scale trading?
2. Is the strategy simple to execute?

Let's first address simplicity of execution. The importance of this factor cannot be overstated. If the plan for reducing drawdowns is too elaborate, requires too much attention to the market, or in some other way is difficult to put in place, it may not be practical. If that's the case, traders may not even use the strategy; or if they do, they may actually get a result opposite from what they are looking for, increasing losses rather than reducing them.

Consider the following idea, proposed in another scale trading book: Implement your scale trades in the traditional way, but if the price drops below the lowest price in your scale, immediately sell short—in another contract month—the number of contracts equivalent to what you have already bought. For example, if you used the scale in Figure 14.1 and April cattle futures dropped below $57 per hundredweight, you would immediately sell eight contracts of another month (say, June) at the market. Why eight? Because at $57 you would have just bought your eighth contract of April cattle. The idea is to control your capital needs by locking in the price at no lower than $57.

This is a good idea under certain circumstances. Had you been scaling cattle in 1996 when June futures went down to $54, you definitely would have had a smaller drawdown if you had shorted another contract month once prices dropped below $57. The creator of this method said that once you are short, you should set a stop on those contracts at your entry point. That might have worked well in 1996, but here is where we run into that problem of simplicity of execution. What happens if you get short eight contracts at or near the low and prices start shooting up? Now, instead of reducing your drawdown, you may increase it by taking a loss on those eight short contracts. When do you get out of those shorts? If you take them out at a loss, do you increase the prices on your scale sells to compensate? The author writes that sometimes the execution of his method reminds him of when he used to be a fighter pilot attempting to land on the deck of a carrier. This method seems too hard to work consistently.

Another possibility would be to just get out of your longs instead of selling short another contract month. This solves nothing because you

RECOMMENDED SCALE TRADE PLAN

Commodity: Live Cattle
Month: April
Starting price: $67.50
Maintenance Margin: $425
Profit/loss per $: $400.00
Buy-down increment: $1.50
Sell-profit increment: $1.00 $400
Total buy levels: 8
Contracts at each level: 1

1				2				3	4	5	6	7	8
Buy Level	Buy Price	Date Order Placed	Date Order Filled	Sell Price	Date Order Placed	Date Order Filled	No. of Contracts Held	Losing Contracts	Loss per Contract	Possible Cumulative Loss per Contract	Possible Cumulative Loss on All Contracts	Cumulative Required Margin	Minimum Account Funds
1	$67.50			$68.50			1	0	$ 0.00	$ 0.00	$ 0.00	$ 425.00	$ 425.00
2	66.00			67.00			2	1	600.00	600.00	600.00	850.00	1,450.00
3	64.50			65.50			3	2	600.00	1,200.00	1,800.00	1,275.00	3,075.00
4	63.00			64.00			4	3	600.00	1,800.00	3,600.00	1,700.00	5,300.00
5	61.50			62.50			5	4	600.00	2,400.00	6,000.00	2,125.00	8,125.00
6	60.00			61.00			6	5	600.00	3,000.00	9,000.00	2,550.00	11,550.00
7	58.50			59.50			7	6	600.00	3,600.00	12,600.00	2,975.00	15,575.00
8	57.00			58.00			8	7	600.00	4,200.00	16,800.00	3,400.00	20,200.00

Figure 14.1 April cattle scale. (*Source:* FutureSource/Bridge)

still have the same kind of execution problem: Exactly when do you get back into your scale? Lower prices would be nice, but what about when you get out at the lows and have to reenter at higher prices? Do you move all your sells higher? The problem with that is that it can make sells a little tougher to achieve.

There is another way to approach this problem: Use options. First, we'll take a look at what these tools are and how they work. Then I'll explain a couple of ways to use them in a scale trade.

UNDERSTANDING OPTIONS

Kinds of Options

There are two kinds of options: call and puts. An *option* gives the buyer the right but not the obligation to buy (in the case of a call option) or sell (in the case of a put option) the underlying futures contract at a specific price, known as the *strike* or *exercise price,* by a specific date (the expiration date). The option buyer pays a *premium* for this right (the price of the option), which the option seller receives. But because option buyers are not obligated to exercise their option and buy (in the case of a call) or sell (in the case of a put) the underlying future, their risk on the option is limited to the price they pay for it.

For example, a November soybean call option is the right to buy a November soybean futures contract at a specific price. This price is the strike price, and strike prices are set at fixed intervals. So a November $5 bean call is the right to buy a contract of November beans at $5. A November $5 bean put would be the right to sell a contract of beans at $5.

Figure 14.2 shows a table of the prices for the various November 2000 bean options on a day in June. The calls are on the right, and the puts are on the left. Across the middle of the table, you can find the $5 calls and puts labeled "500." Looking on the right, you can see that the last trade for the $5 calls occurred at a price of 52 cents per bushel ("520s"). To figure out the cost to you, the only information you need is the contract size and the unit size. In the case of beans, the unit size is a bushel, the contract size is 5,000 bushels, and the price is in cents per bushel.

```
FutureSource Technical                                          _ 🗗 ✕
File  Pages  Setup  Flash  Back  <<  >>  Help
```

SS	Up,Down,PgUp,PgDn = More. Left,Right = Headings. ESC when done												
	Puts						Calls					15:14
	Str	Bid	Ask	High	Low	Last	Str	Bid	Ask	High	Low	Last
XO	325						XO 325			2074	2074	2074s
XO	350						XO 350			1824	1700	1824s
XO	375			4	4	4s	XO 375					
XO	400			10	10	10s	XO 400			1334	1290	1334s
XO	425	20		23	5	23s	XO 425					
XO	450			54	42	52s	XO 450			870	870	870s
XO	475			114	104	104s	XO 475			670	650	670s
XO	500			206	184	196s	XO 500			520	494	520s
XO	525			334	320	324s	XO 525			400	300	400s
XO	550			494	480	480s	XO 550			320	280	304s
XO	575			664	660	660s	XO 575			250	230	240s
XO	600			854	854	854s	XO 600			196	170	190s
XO	625			1060	1060	1060s	XO 625			156	140	150s
XO	650			1290	1290	1290s	XO 650			134	114	125s
XO	675			1520	1520	1520s	XO 675			102	94	102s
XO	700						XO 700			94	82	86s
							XO 725	84		74	74	74s
XO	750						XO 750			62	60	62s
XO	800						XO 800			44	36	44s
							XO 850			32	30	32s

v More v

Figure 14.2 Soybean options price table. (*Source:* FutureSource/Bridge)

(An interesting aside for newcomers is the way in which exchanges arrived at contract sizes: A commodity future is almost always a railroad car full of that commodity—5,000 bushels in a grain contract; 1,000 barrels of oil in a crude oil contract; 40,000 pounds of cattle in a cattle contract. There are exceptions, for instance, a 50-ounce contract of platinum. Despite the exceptions, old-timers still refer to a futures contract as a "car," as in a railroad car. This term is even applied to Standard & Poor's (S&P) 500 Index futures, bond futures, and platinum futures. So, if you hear someone saying you bought two cars of something, you now know what they are referring to.)

Value of Options

To get the value of the $5 November bean call, all you need do is multiply the price of 52 cents per bushel by the 5,000 bushels in a contract, which comes out to $2,600. That's what a $5 November bean call would have cost on that June day. If beans fail to climb above $5 by option expiration in October, then your option will expire worthless. Between the time you purchase the option and the time when it expires, you can sell the option at a profit, if available, or at a loss.

How does the market determine what the price of an option should be? The value of an option is determined the same way the value of a futures contract is determined—how much is someone willing to pay for it? Just as with futures, there is an auction for each option, and the value of each option tends to fluctuate each day. Many factors affect what the market is willing to pay for an option. Options can get pretty complicated, but the most important factors are how close an option's strike price is to the current price of the futures and how much time there is until the option expires.

There are two types of value in an option: *intrinsic* value and *extrinsic* value. Intrinsic value is the amount an option is said to be "in the money." A call option is in the money if the underlying futures price is higher than the strike price of the option. A put option is in the money if the price of the underlying futures is below the strike price of the put. The intrinsic value of an in-the-money option is the difference between the strike price and the current futures price. An out-of-the-money option would have zero intrinsic value, so any value that it has is extrinsic.

If you own a $5 November bean call and the underlying futures price is $5.08, your call option is 8 cents in the money and, therefore, has an 8-cent intrinsic value. If the market price of that option is 31 cents, the remaining 23 cents is extrinsic value. Extrinsic value is sometimes referred to as premium. Admittedly, this is confusing because the term *premium* is also used to refer to the whole price for an option. In this discussion I want to focus on the use of the word *premium* to denote that portion of the option price that is extrinsic.

Premium is determined by the marketplace based on a number of factors, but the most important are volatility and time to expiration. A very quiet market will not tend to command a high premium because it is less likely that an option buyer will profit. A very volatile market makes it seem more likely that a buyer of a given option will profit. So that kind of market tends to command higher premiums. Because scale traders are buying into falling markets that are already somewhat depressed, the typical option a scale trader will encounter will be of the low-volatility type. Because our plan is to be able to execute in any type of market, we will ignore volatility in our considerations. More sophisticated traders may choose to do otherwise, but for the purpose of this book I would like to focus on a method I can use at any time.

For now, I would like to focus on time to expiration. An option is valued according to how much it is in or out of the money, the volatility of the market, and how much time is left to option expiration. Each day that goes by is one day less that an option has left to get into the money. Therefore, the part of the option premium related to time declines every day, a factor known as *time decay*. If the November bean futures that were at $4.97 in August stayed at that price until the November options expired on October 23, then the value of the $5 November bean call option would have declined each day until expiration, at which point the option would expire worthless. If I bought this option on August 10 and paid 31 cents for the $5 call, that 31 cents is now a cost factor to me. Therefore, what I really want is for the price to get above $5.31 to pay for the premium and to ensure a profit. Because each day that goes by represents less time left for this to happen, each day the option is worth a little less.

Because of time decay, options are sometimes referred to as a *wasting asset,* much like a new car. Each day you own it, it is worth a little less until it eventually expires worthless. An out-of-the-money option expires worthless because it has no intrinsic value and all of its extrinsic value has disappeared. If an option expires in the money, it will be worth precisely the amount by which it is in the money. So if we buy a November $5 bean call for 31 cents and November beans are at $5.08 at expiration, our call option would only be worth 8 cents. We would have lost 23 cents worth of premium.

USING PUT OPTIONS

Let's go back to the execution problem we talked about earlier in the chapter when we discussed either selling short in another contract month or moving out of our contracts as a way of limiting drawdowns. We concluded that the execution of that type of strategy was very likely too difficult to make it practical. One way to simplify the execution problem would be to buy put options.

Because a put is an option on a short sale, it increases in value when the price of futures drops. Thus, you could use puts to lock in the bottom of your scale. Because the loss on an option you have bought is limited to the cost of the option, you also wouldn't have the concern about exactly when to get out of your puts. By contrast, if prices go up indefinitely and you are short in another contract month, as in the method proposed earlier, you could keep losing indefinitely on your shorts. Using options instead, your loss would be limited to the cost of the option premium; once prices rose enough to compensate for the loss of the option premium, you would be free to make money on your longs.

The drawback of this approach is that, because you have to pay for options, you are in the position of having to overcome those costs once prices start to rise. As a result, you must account for this in your overall scale plan. This may be possible, but it would mean seeking larger profits per contract and making oscillations less likely. In a straight down-and-up market, this approach will work great; but in a choppy market, you may wish you didn't have those puts.

USING CALL OPTIONS

Another possibility is scaling with *call options* instead of futures contracts. The advantage of this approach is that it provides a clear definition of the risk. But there are disadvantages as well.

Because of time decay, scale trading using call options at each buy point on the way down is a difficult way to make money. The futures not only have to come up, but they have to come up enough to overcome any time decay that the options are experiencing while you are waiting. The likely loss of return from this method seems unacceptable.

There may be another way to use options that could be very acceptable. What if you could use the time decay of options to your advantage? In the same way that you can buy or sell a futures contract, you can buy or sell options. If you sell an option short, the pressure of time decay can work in your favor.

This is precisely the strategy I propose: selling short the premium of an option. First, you buy each contract in a scale as you normally would. What is different is that each time you buy a futures contract, you sell short a call option against it. Let's take a typical scale and see how it would work, using the January platinum scale from Chapter 11 for our scale (Figure 14.3).

When you buy at $350 an ounce, instead of placing a sell order at $360, you sell short a January call. On August 10, 1999, the $360 January platinum calls were trading at $10.60. A platinum contract is 50 ounces, so $10.60 is equal to $530 ($10.60 × 50). If you sell short the $360 January call, you add $530 to your account balance. Each day the value of the option shows up as a liability and, as such, is deducted from the net value of your account until either you buy it back or it expires. If it expires worthless, the $530 is yours to keep. Let's see how this approach would work in various scale trade scenarios.

- *Scenario 1:* You buy platinum at $350, and it goes steadily down for the next few months, eventually declining to shocking lows in the $280s. Along the way you buy a contract at $350, another at $340, one at $330, and so on, down to $290, at which time you have seven contracts. The capital required for this scale when the price is at $290 is $18,200. If you are able to collect an average of $500 per call option sold on the way down, you are potentially reducing your drawdown by $3,500. (This is before you have dropped below the lowest buy in your scale.) If you're concerned that the price might drop a lot lower, you could use this money to buy puts at $280 or lower to keep you from greatly increasing that drawdown if prices keep dropping.

- *Scenario 2:* You start a scale in platinum at $350 and the price bounces around, going down to $330 and up as high as $360 before dropping back to $330. Having sold call options along the way, you don't want to oscillate in and out. Any time you sell a contract, you must buy back the short call options. Otherwise, you would be left with naked short call options, which, without being long the underlying futures, become a liability. Rising futures prices result in rising call option prices, which means a short call option will lose money. This is not a problem if you are long the underlying futures contract, and, as we will see, it can even be an advantage. But if you sell the underlying futures contract and continue to hold a short call option, the call option then becomes a very risky position. I do not recommend doing that unless you are a very experienced option seller (and maybe not even then).

RECOMMENDED SCALE TRADE PLAN

Commodity	Platinum
Month	July
Starting price	$360.00
Maintenance margin	$1,100.00
Profit/loss per $	$50.00
Buy-down increment	$5.00
Sell-profit increment	$10.00
Total buy levels	7
Contracts at each level	1

PLEASE REMEMBER THAT COMMODITY TRADING INVOLVES A HIGH DEGREE OF LEVERAGE. THAT LEVERAGE ALLOWS FOR LARGE RETURNS BUT ALSO LARGE LOSSES. DUE TO THE HIGH DEGREE OF RISK INVOLVED IN HIGH LEVERAGE, YOU SHOULD CAREFULLY CONSIDER WHETHER COMMODITY TRADING IS APPROPRIATE FOR YOU. AS ALWAYS, MARKET CONDITIONS MAY MAKE IT DIFFICULT, IF NOT IMPOSSIBLE, TO EXECUTE ORDERS.

Buy Level	Buy Price	Sell Price	No. of Contracts Held	Losing Contracts	Loss per Contract	Possible Cumulative Loss per Contract	Possible Cumulative Loss on All Contracts	Cumulative Required Margin	Minimum Account Funds
	1		2	3	4	5	6	7	8
1	$360.00	$370.00	1	0	$ 0.00	$ 0.00	$ 0.00	$1,100.00	$ 1,100.00
2	355.00	365.00	2	1	250.00	250.00	250.00	2,200.00	2,450.00
3	350.00	360.00	3	2	250.00	500.00	750.00	3,300.00	4,050.00
4	345.00	355.00	4	3	250.00	750.00	1,500.00	4,400.00	5,900.00
5	340.00	350.00	5	4	250.00	1,000.00	2,500.00	5,500.00	8,000.00
6	335.00	345.00	6	5	250.00	1,250.00	3,750.00	6,600.00	10,350.00
7	330.00	340.00	7	6	250.00	1,500.00	5,250.00	7,700.00	12,950.00

Figure 14.3 Platinum scale.

This becomes a different kind of trade. If you try to hold a short call option without the underlying futures contract, you have changed from being a scale trader to being an options trader. Only do this if you are clear that that is what you want to do and if you know what you are doing with short options. Because this book is about scale trading, I will continue on the assumption that you will not trade naked short options but will instead liquidate them promptly when you sell the underlying futures contract. Each time you buy a futures contract in your scale and then sell a call option against it, your position is known as a *covered call*. When looking to take a profit on this kind of trade, you will need to take into consideration the value of the call. You will likely take a loss on the call option, so you will need to make enough of a profit on the underlying futures to overcome the loss on the call option.

The factor that comes into play here is known as *delta,* the Greek letter used to represent rate of change in mathematical formulas. When applied to options, delta represents the rate of change in the value of an option relative to the change in the value of the underlying futures contract, expressed as a percentage. The maximum value for the delta of an option is 1.00, which is 100%. A delta of 1.00 means that the option value would change at the same rate as the underlying futures contract. For example, if a platinum call option has a delta of 1.00 and platinum rallies $10, then we would expect the platinum call option to increase $10 as well. A platinum call option with a delta of .50 would rally $5 if the platinum futures rallied $10.

As previously stated, a call option is in the money when the price of the underlying futures contract is above the strike price of the option. A $360 platinum call would be in the money when the price of the futures is above $360. When the futures are at $360, the option is said to be *at the money.* Many factors determine the delta of an option, but none is more important than how much the option is in or out of the money. A deep-in-the-money option will approach a delta of 1.00, while a deep-out-of-the-money option will approach a delta of zero. Because all options have to be assigned a value, it is technically impossible for an option to get to zero delta until it has expired, but it can get pretty close.

At-the-money options generally have a delta of about .50. This, along with the time decay of options, helps the scale trader. That's because an option with a delta of .50 will only move about 50 percent of any move in the underlying futures contract.

Now, I'd like to stop here and make a point that all these numbers I'm throwing about are not only hypothetical but also a little rough. To really nail it down—and there are legions of people at institutions who do this—you need to factor in a whole lot of other things. I'm not going to get into all that other stuff because for our purposes rough estimates will do the job. But I am aware that many readers are highly intelligent people, have extensive experience in options, or both. If you fit either of those descriptions, you may be wondering, "If the delta of an at-the-money option is 50 percent and the price rises, won't the delta increase make it difficult for me to profit by selling at-the-money options?" The answer is yes, but as the price increases and the intrinsic value increases, the premium is decreasing. As the premium decreases, you make money because you are short the premium. When you are long the futures and short an at-the-money call option, you are essentially neutral the intrinsic value of the option. All your money is made on the deterioration of the option premium.

Therefore, you only want to sell options with a large enough premium to be worthwhile. I would certainly hesitate to sell an option with a premium below $400. In the platinum options example, I have sold an out-of-the-money call. The preceding example had us buying the futures at $350 and selling a $360 call for $530. This is a great situation because we have a full $10 to go before our call option is at the money, and we still get a $530 premium for selling it. If you can sell slightly out-of-the-money options for that kind of premium, you may find things working much better because the delta on the out-of-the-money $360 call is going to be lower than the delta on the at-the-money $350 call. If prices advance $10 to $360 and the $350 call has a delta of .50, the $350 call would advance by about $5 (.50 × $10). Meanwhile, if the delta on the $360 call were .35, then the price on the $360 call would advance by about $3.50, or $175 in value. At the same time, if we bought the futures at $350, the futures will have increased in value by $10, or $500 in value.

See how this all works in your favor? Clearly, we haven't made as much money as we would have if we had just bought the futures in the traditional way. That's the drawback here. And the drag of these options makes oscillations less likely. Generally speaking, you have to make twice as much on the futures to overcome the drag of the short call options.

It all comes down to choosing the type of risk with which you are most comfortable. If you choose a defensive strategy, choose one with costs and risks that work for you. My choice is to use traditional scaling, but occasionally, especially when the premiums are fat, I will write call options against my scale purchases. I prefer this to buying puts to protect myself because, even though puts give me more certainty, they cost money that may end up wasted. Writing options may also produce a drag on the account if I am taking losses on those positions, but the additional capital sure comes in handy when the occasional scale drops far below my expectations.

15

DON'T SKIP THIS CHAPTER: CHOOSING A BROKER

I titled this chapter "Don't Skip This Chapter" because a lot of people don't realize how important this subject is. I have been in the brokerage business since 1987, and, trust me, there's a lot you need to know. You may already have a broker with whom you feel you are satisfied, but if he or she doesn't meet the criteria laid out in this chapter, I would strongly suggest you give serious thought to finding another broker.

SECURITY

Security should be the first area to consider when choosing a broker. Very few people consider how safe their money is when they deposit it with a broker. Few people would even think about putting money in a bank that wasn't insured by the Federal Deposit Insurance Corporation (FDIC). Stock brokerage accounts are protected by the Securities Investor Protection Corporation (SIPC), but commodity accounts have no such insurance. Instead, the exchanges maintain an emergency fund to protect customer accounts.

When I tell people this, they are often shocked. People just assume that their money is safe. This could be a very costly assumption.

Your broker may work for a company (Introducing Broker, or IB) who introduces business to a clearing house (Futures Commission Merchant, or FCM) and uses the FCM to place trades.

Clearing houses may be "member" FCMs or "nonmember" FCMs. FCMs, in turn, place their trades in physical locations called "exchanges," such as the Chicago Mercantile Exchange (CME). The exchange provides the facilities and the regulations within which the FCMs trade orders placed by brokers such as your broker.

Nonmember FCMs are halfway between being an IB and an FCM. They handle all the considerable paperwork involved in a trade, but they do not actually make the trade on the floor. They contract a member FCM to actually place the trade.

Accounts of member FCMs are protected by the exchange of which they are a member. Instead of insurance, the exchanges maintain an emergency fund to protect the accounts of their members. The Chicago Mercantile Exchange, for instance, has almost $100 million in its emergency fund. From time to time, FCMs do go bankrupt. If the FCM is a member, the exchange will provide the cash necessary to guarantee the customer positions in the market and, if necessary, the cash in the customer accounts.

Although numerous FCMs have gone bankrupt, there has never been a bankruptcy of a commodity exchange in the history of the United States, not even in the great depression. And no customer of a member FCM has ever lost money due to a member FCM's bankruptcy.

That's a wonderful record, one with which I feel very comfortable as I deposit my money with a member FCM. If my account is with a nonmember FCM, the story may be different: Exchanges would guarantee my positions but not my cash. My money is deposited into a customer-segregated account. According to the Commodity Exchange Act, these funds are supposed to be protected from creditors. In practice, this has worked very well, and you do not need to lie awake at night worrying about it. However, if you have the choice between a member FCM and a nonmember FCM, take the member.

All this discussion may be just splitting hairs, and it is in the book primarily for your information; but I would consider this as a factor when choosing between FCMs.

There are some more important factors on the issue of security. One is the amount of capitalization. All FCMs are required to maintain a certain amount of minimum capital relative to the amount of customer deposits. Most firms maintain amounts close to or a little above their required amount.

This is a bit of an oversimplification, but you can judge firms just by looking at the absolute amount of capital and not worry too much about how much excess capital they have over their minimum required amount. If Company A has $4 million in capital and Company B has $80 million in capital, I'm more interested in having my money with Company B. I just figure that Company B has a lot more money to go through before it would be bankrupt than Company A does.

Those of you with accounting backgrounds may want to dig deeper. If you do, have fun. Ask for the firm's balance sheet. Ask for its capital requirement. You wonderful folks who like to do that kind of thing will be better informed than the rest of us. If you are like me, just stick with the firms that have the higher numbers. They tend to have more longevity than those with the small numbers.

FCM SERVICE

Another thing to look for is the number of exchanges of which the FCM or clearing house is a member. There are many exchanges in the United States and around the world. Membership in one may not give a firm the privileges of membership in the rest. I'm principally concerned about floor service here. I have never seen a clearing firm that didn't make the claim that they had "superior order execution." They never say superior to what. It's a vague claim that really says nothing and they all use it.

One clue as to what kind of execution you are going to get is whether they are a member of all the exchanges on which you will be trading. If they are not a member of a given exchange, the chances are you will find yourself getting consistently poor service on that exchange. This is not necessarily always true, but it is a pretty fair rule of thumb.

How will you know if you are getting poor service? As a scale trader, you will only use limit orders. This eliminates the bane of many a trader—slippage. *Slippage* is what happens when you have a stop order that is executed at a worse price than specified. For example, suppose you have a stop to sell soybeans at $5.05. Your broker notifies you that your order has been filled at $5.03. Why? A stop order becomes a market order as soon as the price is touched. So if the market is moving rapidly when it trades at your stop price, you will normally be filled at a worse price than you specified. This is known as slippage, and it is very aggravating because it costs traders money. Poor service most often comes in the form of excessive slippage.

A more subtle and more important area to scale traders comes at the high or the low of the day. It's rare, but every once in a while you will have a limit order to buy at the low of the day or to sell at the high of the day. If you are getting good service, you will get filled at these places something like 25 percent to 65 percent of the time—the more often, the better the service. Poor service means you are never getting the high or the low of the day.

As a scale trader, this can be very important to you. Suppose you are scaling hogs and the low of the day is $39.00 and you have an order to buy at $39.00. Let's further suppose that the low at $39.00 on that day is the lowest price for a month and the price subsequently rallies up to $40.50. If you don't get filled at $39.00, you just missed a profit. If you were taking 100-point profits on your hog scale, poor service cost you $400.

REGULATORY HISTORY

The kind of regulatory history that the broker and his company have is another consideration when you are evaluating a broker. You've been talking to someone on the phone, and he seems like a good guy. Is he really? There is an easy way to check. Contact the regulatory agencies. Unfortunately, this won't tell you everything you would like to know, but it can be a big help in the right circumstances.

Check with the National Futures Association (NFA). This is the self-regulatory body of the futures industry. It is the enforcer. The NFA operates under the authority of the Commodity Futures Trading Commission (CFTC), an agency of the federal government. The CFTC sets policies and regulations, and the NFA is the agency that enforces most of them.

You can call the NFA at 1-800-621-3570. When the very helpful clerk answers the phone, tell him or her that you would like to check on an individual and a firm. The clerk will then verify whether that individual and firm are properly registered. This is important because it means you are dealing with legitimate people rather than some kind of scam artists posing as brokers. The clerk will then check to see whether there have been any disciplinary actions against the broker and the firm. Ideally, you would like to find no actions. This doesn't mean you are dealing with honest people. It just means they have never been caught doing anything that was very wrong.

The flip side of this is the same. If they have been cited for doing something wrong, it doesn't mean they are bad guys. It may just mean they tripped up somewhere. There are so many regulations in this business that it is difficult to keep them all straight. But if the broker has a long list of actions against him or her, I would forget about that broker.

The firm is another story. Brokerages deal with even more regulations than individuals and are scrutinized more closely. They tend to have been around longer and have done many, many times more business than any individual. In the course of doing that much business, it is natural that somewhere along the line they would slip up or have someone complain sometime. I tend to get a little glassy-eyed looking over the list of infractions that most brokerages have. It's very difficult to tell the minor ones from the major ones. You might not get an answer, but try asking the clerk if he thinks the brokerage is one of the good guys or one of the bad guys. They're not supposed to answer a question like that, but if you ask nicely, you might get an answer.

You can also look up much of this information yourself by going to the NFA Web site at www.nfa.futures.org. On the homepage, click on the link that says BASIC for Background Affiliation Status Information Center. You can then enter the name of the broker or the firm to get any information the NFA has on them if they are registered with the NFA.

BROKERAGE SERVICES

Now let's look at some of the services a broker might perform for you. One of the most important services is market information and research. I'm not referring to trade recommendations. As scale traders, we really are not interested in the buy/sell recommendations of brokers. I'm not sure we're interested in them at any time. I have a saying: "Those who know how to trade, trade; those who don't, write newsletters; and those who really don't, become brokers."*

---

*Author's note: Since I published the original version of this book in 1997, a couple of commentators have taken offense at this last statement and wondered if I even realized that, because I am a broker, I am putting myself down here. I stand by my statement. Making a living as a trader is the hardest thing to do in this business. Making

Please remember that I have been a broker since 1987. Most of the other brokers I know can't trade to save their lives. Some of my competitors actually call me to ask my opinion on markets. That always surprises me, but I guess it shouldn't. Most brokers are salespeople, not analysts or traders.

I don't mean to denigrate my peers, but all you have to do is think about what the job of a broker is all about. It is extremely rare that a broker walks into a situation where he or she is given a clientele. Almost all brokers have to go out and find their own clients. Brokers are the salespeople of the industry. Once they have clients, they are required to service those clients. Most really don't know how, so they rely on newsletters and company research. But remember, newsletter writers and researchers do not trade for a living. If their recommendations don't make money, it doesn't cost them anything. If they lose subscribers because of it, they just advertise for new ones.

I once visited a very well known brokerage. The owner of this brokerage has written a famous book on commodities, and he writes a widely followed newsletter. I spoke to his sales manager (please note that the person who manages the brokers is referred to as the *sales* manager). I asked him what the success rate of his clients was. Specifically, I asked, "Our industry has a problem. The customers don't make money. How are things here? Are your customers doing any better?" His answer was, "I'd like to say that our customers do better. If they do, it's maybe only one percent or two percent better."

In other words, if 95 percent of everybody else's clients lose money, he was saying that 93 percent or 94 percent was the best he might hope for at his company. He went on to talk about how they try to structure a funnel for their brokers—more coming in the top than going out the bottom—and that they do this with massive advertising to keep lots of fresh customers coming in the door.

This story is more than a lesson about brokers. It is also a lesson about scale traders. Our company, Crown Futures Corporation, does

---

a living as a newsletter writer is not easy but it is easier than making it as a trader. Making a living as a broker is the easiest by far, though not necessarily easy. Most of my peers are salespeople. A few of my peers are very good brokers who are quite knowledgeable about markets. My intent here, however, is not to put anyone down but rather to help the reader find the kind of sources and relationships that will help him or her in trading. Toward that end, my somewhat poking-fun statement is really just saying, "Caveat emptor."

not advertise aggressively. We do want to grow, but we are literally afraid of getting overloaded with new accounts because we are so busy with our existing accounts. That's because we specialize in scale trading. The point here is not that Crown Futures Corporation is such a great company (of course, I believe it is—I run it!), but that scale traders do not have the same types of experience that the typical commodity customer has. If the scale trader did, we would have to advertise more frequently or try to find another methodology that would work with similar results to scale trading.

I wonder what would happen if commodity brokerages were not allowed to advertise. It seems to me that in less than a year most brokerages would be out of business. Is that any way to run an investment business?

Does all of this sad story about brokers mean you should never listen to your broker? No. Your broker does have valuable information for you about the markets you wish to scale. As I discussed in Chapter 4, your broker can bring you fundamental research and information that may be hard to get elsewhere.

Most important, remember what I said about brokers. Don't just accept your broker's analysis. He or she may know more than you do, but it still may be a whole lot less than you need. We're hoping that your broker is a conduit of good fundamental research from good analysts. If you read the chapters in this book on fundamental analysis carefully, you may at least know what it looks like when you see it.

A good broker can bring you invaluable information that you can use to be a more successful scale trader. But information, although extremely important, is not enough.

At this point you know a lot about the broker you are considering. Let's briefly review what you know:

1. You know something about the broker's level of integrity by having checked with the regulators for any problems in his or her or the firm's past.

2. You know something about the financial stability of the company through which he or she clears trades and at which your money will be deposited.

3. You have a guess about the kind of floor service you can expect.

   4. You have a good idea about the kind of information you can expect to receive from him or her.

That's quite a lot, but you still need to know a little more. First, you need to know if you can get along with this person. Getting along with your broker is very important. The last thing you want is someone who is zigging when you're zagging. This is subjective, but if you've been gathering all the information about your broker as just discussed, you've probably spent some time talking with him or her on the phone.

By now you have an idea whether you like this person. We're not talking about popularity contests. Some very bad brokers seem like very nice people, so I definitely am not advocating picking a person because he or she seems like the nicest person. You need to at least have a belief that you can get along with this person. If you are always going to be at odds with your broker, your success is likely to be hindered.

Second, you need to know how much scale trading experience he or she has. Most brokers don't like scale trading because scale traders tend to put positions on that stay there for months. Brokers like you to turn your positions over more frequently than that—preferably several times a day. I'm not kidding! The more often you trade, the more income they make on the same money. So a position that just sits there for months is anathema to most brokers.

Experienced scale trade brokers have an entirely different outlook. This is what you are looking for. Their outlook is long term. The critical thing to them is that the client makes money. As long as the client makes money, commissions will be there in ever-increasing amounts. The experienced scale trade broker knows that scale trading will accomplish this for him or her.

The experienced scale trade broker will have developed in-house systems for dealing with the unique requirements of scale traders. Unlike other traders, scale traders tend to have large amounts of good-'til-canceled (GTC) orders, which presents a problem because a GTC order has to be verified as still being a good order every day. Every day the order desks from each clearing house call up to verify every GTC to see if it is still good.

Please imagine for a moment what this is like. If you have three scales operating, you might have as many as 25 or 30 GTC orders just for your scales. At our company, Crown Futures Corporation, we have well over a hundred customers engaged in scale trading. As I write this, we have approximately 2,100 GTC orders. The desk we use at one clearing house tells us that we have more GTC orders than all the other brokerages using their desk combined! When you consider the amount of work in verifying these orders and then consider that commissions on scale trade accounts tend to be low overall because they don't trade very often, it is no surprise that most brokers are not eager to encourage this type of trading.

You might wonder how we have solved this problem at Crown Futures. The answer is unimportant to you as a scale trader, and I am not going to reveal it because it is a trade secret. Sorry! This book will be read by some of our competitors. It has taken us years to develop effective systems for handling scale trade accounts. We have done this because we believe 100 percent in scale trading. Other brokers will either need to solve these problems on their own or leave the scale trading to us. I certainly hope they choose the latter course. But I want you to know what kind of problems scale trading creates for brokers so you can get a feeling for the value of using an experienced scale trade broker.

COMMISSIONS

How important are commissions? It depends on the type of trading you are doing. To the scale trader, commissions are not an important ingredient to success; scale traders have a profit objective of $200 to $500 per trade. With that kind of objective, whether you pays $20 or $50, the $30 difference will hardly be noticed. (Of course, if the scale trader closes out of his or her scale early or does not stick to the plan, a loss per trade might be experienced.)

Commissions are of far greater importance when you are dealing with systems of marginal profitability or those that lose money altogether. If your method has an average profit per trade of $100, the difference between a deep discount commission of $20 and a full-service commission of $50 is significant, especially if you trade quite frequently, the way a day trader might.

But when you trade far less frequently and your holding period may extend to months, the difference in commissions becomes insignificant. When you consider all the things a good full-service broker can do for you, there really is no question about whether to use a full-service broker or a discount broker. Stick to full service.

Full-Service Broker versus Discount Broker

In thinking of discount brokers, I am reminded of what Sir Francis Bacon said: "There will always be someone who is willing to make something a little worse and sell it for a little less." This is certainly true of discount brokers. You do not get an experienced broker on the other end of the line; you get an entry-level order clerk.

I have been told that one large discount firm runs an ad in the help-wanted section of the *Chicago Tribune* every day. This is not because they are growing fast; it is because of high turnover. If you ask a question of this type of broker, the most frequent answer you will get is, "I don't know." In fact, they are trained to answer almost all questions that way, and a good thing, too. The last thing you want is an answer from someone who knows almost nothing about commodity futures.

As consumers we are always looking for bargains, but sometimes the lowest price is not the best price. Occasionally, by paying a little more, we get a lot more for our money. One example would be staying at a nice hotel with pool, sauna, and continental breakfast versus staying at a cheap roadside motel. The enormous growth of Holiday Inn, Marriott, La Quinta, and so on, is testimony to the fact that we will pay a little more to get more service. This is the role of the full-service broker. The full-service broker can give you important information, experience, and management services that are just not available at a discount firm, and you pay about the difference between staying at a roadhouse and staying at Ramada.

Online Brokers

When I published the first edition of this book in 1997, there were no online brokerage services for commodity traders. Today they are all over. Brokerage houses like online accounts because they involve less work. An online account is a "do-it-yourself" account. When an online trader places an order, it goes directly to the trading floor and bypasses one or more layers of brokers that would normally relay this order. This is a tremendous savings. The nature of competition is that discounters are passing much of that savings on to the public.

The question is, should you as a scale trader use an online account? To answer that question, you need to decide a few things about yourself and your trading. The first thing, I guess, would be obvious. If you are technophobic, you aren't going to want an online account anyway, so no problem. Also, everything I wrote above about discount brokers applies to online brokers.

There is also the matter of contingency orders. Whether at a discount firm or an online firm, contingency orders are not allowed. Contingency orders are very useful to scale traders. A contingency order is simply an "if, then" order: "If I buy copper at 82 cents on my account, then please enter an order to sell copper at 82.75 cents GTC." You can't enter an order like this either online or at a discount house. So if you bought copper at 82 cents in the morning and it went up to 83 cents and back down to 82 cents by the end of the day, either you had to be on top of it yourself or you just missed an oscillation trade. Just missing a few of these could cost you much more money than the difference between a full-service broker and a discount/online firm.

On the other hand, if you are able to stay on top of the market all of the time, then you might find an online account useful. Still, I guess I wonder why a scale trader would want to. One of the beauties of scale trading is that once you set up your scale with the help of a scale trading broker, you can have it run on automatic pilot and just check in for the major decisions about rollovers and the scales to go into. Because your trades would occur automatically, I guess I can't see why you would want to be involved in every one of them to make sure you don't miss any oscillation trades. It seems much more relaxing to me to let a good broker handle it for me. A full-service broker can take contingency orders, and contingency orders are the backbone of efficient scale trading because they allow the broker to get your next order in quickly, making sure you don't miss any of those valuable oscillations.

The main feature of online trading seems to be speed—how fast your order gets to the floor. If I am day trading, that is very important to me. I want to have live quotes and to get my orders in now, especially market orders. But as a scale trader, all this is meaningless. The only time I have need for speed is to get the next order in when I have a buy or a sell so I don't miss a potential oscillation.

That can be done faster without the client's involvement through contingency orders.

Another factor here is that online trading is still fairly primitive. Our firm uses it, and I can tell you that the systems go down frequently. We have access to three different online systems. Sometimes they go down at the exchange, and everybody's online access goes down. Sometimes it is the server, and that could be the server for the clearing house, their Internet service provider (ISP), or your ISP. Even with access to three systems, I would estimate that more than 75 percent of our orders go in by phone. That is hardly because we are technophobic. Rather, it is because the phone is still more reliable and even faster sometimes than online systems.

I have been asking my friends who are professional traders, either for their own account, as fund managers, or for commercial concerns, what they use for their order entry. *Take note here please:* As of early 2000 the answers have all been "phoning a broker." Recent TV commercials would like you to believe that online trading will give you the same edge that professionals have. If that is so, why are the professionals I know using the phone? Their answers vary, but mostly it seems to be about relationships and information. With an online account you don't have anyone working for you out there, gathering information and getting your orders in under the best possible circumstances.

I expect that eventually technology will improve to the point that the quality of online trading will become more attractive to professional traders. When it does, I plan to know about it and use it. For now, I place most of my orders the way that the top traders I know place them.

One More Word about Commissions

I have heard the argument that commissions are relative—if you are losing money, any commission you pay is too much; if you are making money after commissions, then the commission is not too high, no matter what it is. Flawless logic. There's only one problem with it. That argument is usually put forth by high-priced brokers who charge $100 per round-turn or more. The problem here is that if you buy the argument, then you have to pay those high commissions for awhile to find out whether it's too much or not. Better to engage in a little logical thinking of your own first.

Although it is true that as long as you make a decent profit it doesn't matter what you paid in commissions, the fact is that the higher the commissions, the less likely it is that you will profit. This is because it gets harder and harder to overcome the costs of trading.

So when I recommend that you use a good full-service broker, I am recommending that you use one with reasonable commissions. As a scale trader, you don't need or want the discount firm. You are willing to pay a little more to get a lot more service from a good full-service broker. But the emphasis here is on the words "a little more." Paying $100 or more per round-turn is just too much, even for scale traders. Commissions in the neighborhood of half that much are appropriate.

Furthermore, if you trade numerous contracts simultaneously, you should get a break on your rate for those trades. If, instead of buying one contract of corn at $2.40, you buy five contracts there and five more at $2.37, then you should get some form of commission-rate reduction from your broker.

INTEREST VERSUS T-BILLS

Let's talk dollars and cents some more. Discount firms do not pay interest on your account. True, they do make Treasury bills (T-bills) available, but most of the time this is not as good as getting interest on your account. Let's say the 90-day T-bill interest rate is 5 percent. T-bills come in $10,000 denominations. If you have a $50,000 account, you don't want to have five T-bills. This is because you cannot use T-bills to cover a deficit—T-bills are not cash. You may use them as collateral for margin requirements but not to cover the reduced value of your account if a position is negative or in deficit.

So, if you are scaling cocoa and you have $50,000 worth of T-bills and nothing more in your account, then when you buy your first contract, your T-bills will cover your margin requirement. However, if the price declines enough, you will have a margin call, even though you have $50,000 worth of T-bills. So on a $50,000 account it is not wise to have more than $40,000 worth of T-bills. Because scale traders want to acquire inventory, it is not all that unusual that a scale trade account would draw down more than 20 percent.

This means that occasionally you will find yourself in the situation where even keeping $10,000 in cash and $40,000 in T-bills won't prevent a margin call. In that case, you would be required either to send in more money or to break a T-bill. All FCMs have charges for breaking a T-bill before maturity that might be more than the interest you have earned on your bill. The main point here is that T-bills are unwieldy because they only come in $10,000 increments and because they can only be used for margin, not for drawdowns.

A better way to earn interest is available through some full-service brokers. This discussion about interest earnings is not trivial. Clearing firms do not like to give interest on accounts. One of the prime ways they earn money is the interest they earn on your money. I have heard it said that one of the largest discount firms just breaks even on commissions and makes all its money on the interest on your money. Interest is not a trivial consideration.

The difference in interest policies from most discount brokers to a good full-service broker may be enough to pay for the difference in commissions. If it works out that way, it would mean you would be able to get a good, hard-working, experienced, full-service broker for the same price as an inexperienced, uninformed, discount-order desk clerk. This is one of the great bargains in investment services if you are careful to get the right interest policy.

Our firm insists that any clearing firm we use for scale traders pays interest on their accounts. The best policy we have gotten from any firm is three-fourths of the T-bill rate on the entire deposit. This is much better than owning T-bills. First of all, under this policy you get interest on every penny of value in your account. Second, there is no risk of having to break any bills.

My recommendation is to stick with a good interest policy. It is almost always better than T-bills.

MARGINS

Another important factor to consider in choosing a broker is margins. Many firms, particularly discount firms, require you to post more than the exchange minimum required margin to make a trade. Some firms will charge as much as double the exchange minimum. This can be critical to a scale trader. If you have to put up more margin, you will be able to scale less on your money than otherwise might have been the case. This goes right to your bottom line because you will have fewer profit opportunities because of it.

You should always insist on getting exchange minimum margins. Make no exceptions. Why would a firm require more than exchange minimum margins? There may be some good reasons for this, but the most cynical one is that they want to make more money in interest on your account. Simply put, if you have to deposit more money in your account to make trades, that's more money on which the firm makes interest. This is a hidden cost, particularly at discount firms. Watch out for it and avoid it.

THANKS

Well, that's all I have to say for now. Thanks for your attention. If you would like a free copy of our scale trading newsletter, call us at 800-634-9650. Check out our Web site at www.ScaleTrading.com.

Good trading to you!

Appendix I

GETTING A HANDLE ON COMMODITY FUTURES: A PRIMER FOR BEGINNING TRADERS

Before delving into the specifics of the scale trading method, it is important to understand the instruments you will be trading with this approach. Reviewing the futures markets (and commodity futures specifically) will give you a better feel for how these instruments behave and why the scale approach is so well suited to trading them.

FUTURES ARE CONTRACTS

A good way to understand futures contracts is to compare them to stocks. When you buy a stock, you are purchasing equity in a company—you own a piece of it, right then and there. When you buy and sell futures, by comparison, you are not really buying or selling anything. What you are doing is entering into an agreement with the person with whom you trade for something you *might* buy or sell later—the reason futures are more precisely referred to as "futures contracts."

When you buy a futures contract, you are agreeing to buy a commodity or a financial instrument (corn, soybeans, crude oil, or Treasury bonds, for example) at a specific price by a specific date in the future. The person on the other side of the trade agrees to sell you ("deliver") that same commodity or financial instrument at the specified price by the specified date. Stories of confused traders waking up to find mountains of corn dumped on their front lawns are jokes; the majority of futures transactions never involve the actual exchange of physical commodities or financial instruments. If you sell your futures contract by a specific date, you offset your position with no further obligations, and you have either profited or lost on the trade itself.

Modern-day commodity futures came into being as a method for farmers who produced and for businesses who used agricultural products to establish centralized markets for raw commodities and to set prices for future transactions. Prices for commodities tended to fluctuate wildly, with no one really able to determine what fair value might be at any given time. Organized futures markets allowed farmers to hedge their crops by selling futures, locking in the price they would receive for their goods at harvest time months in advance. Businesses that used corn, wheat, soybeans, and other commodities for their products also could set the prices they would pay for them.

Unlike stock, which is the same entity month to month and year to year, futures contracts have limited lives and are traded in a regular series of "contract months" (also referred to as "delivery months") that vary from market to market. For example, grain futures at the Chicago Board of Trade (CBOT) have contracts for March, May, July, September, and December. CBOT soybean futures have contracts for January, March, May, July, August, September, and November. If you buy or sell a July 2001 corn futures contract, you are trading corn for delivery in July 2001. If you trade the December 2000 wheat contract, you are trading wheat for delivery in December 2000. All futures contracts have specific expiration dates after which no further trading is allowed.

Multiple contracts for a particular commodity usually trade at the same time, often several years into the future. Corn futures trading may feature as many as a dozen contract months trading two years into the future. For most (but not all) futures markets, active trading is concentrated in the first one or two contract months. The current contract (the one that will expire next) is called the "front month," while the other contracts are referred to as "back months." When the current front month expires, the next month in the cycle becomes the new front month. If you are a long-term trader holding a position spanning more than one contract month, you have to liquidate your position in the current contract month and reestablish your position in the next contract month in the cycle, a process called "rollover." For example, if you bought November 2000 soybean futures and wanted to hold your long position past the end of trading in the November contract, you would simultaneously sell the November futures (before they expired) and buy the January 2001 futures.

COMMODITY GROUPS

Futures markets are traditionally divided into several categories:

- Grains—wheat, corn, soybeans, oats, rice, and so on.
- Meats—cattle, hogs, pork bellies, and so on.
- Softs—other agricultural commodities, such as coffee, sugar and cocoa.
- Metals—gold, silver, copper, platinum, and so on.
- Energies—crude oil, gasoline, heating oil, and so on.
- Financials—stock indexes, such as the Standard & Poor's (S&P) 500, and interest rates, such as Treasury bonds and the Eurodollar.
- Currencies—Japanese yen, Swiss franc, U.S. dollar, and so on.

DELIVERY VERSUS CASH SETTLEMENT

Many futures contracts, mostly financial contracts such as the S&P 500 stock index, are "cash-settled"—they do not have a physical, deliverable underlying commodity. Such futures are simply settled for a cash value on the last day of trading. For example, if you were long the June 1999 S&P futures at 1250 at the close of trading on expiration day and the market settled at 1255, your trading account would be credited with a profit of 5 points, or $1,000.

Positions in deliverable futures (most agricultural, metals, and energy contracts and some financial contracts, such as Treasury bonds) must be liquidated by a specified date (called the "First Notice day") to avoid the risk of making or taking delivery on a physical commodity. Delivery dates (the period of time when the commodity or financial instrument can be physically delivered to fulfill the futures contract) are different in each market, but they usually fall in the final weeks of a contract month. You can easily verify these dates with your broker or the exchange.

CONTRACT SIZES

Futures exchanges determine the size and the quality specifications for their contracts (as well as all the relevant delivery dates and rules). Corn, wheat, and soybeans, for example, trade in contracts of 5,000 bushels at the CBOT. Pork bellies trade in 40,000-pound contracts at the Chicago Mercantile Exchange (CME). If you want to find out how much a futures contract is worth, simply multiply its price by the contract size. For example, if July 1999 wheat is trading at $2.10 a bushel, the value of the contract is $10,500 (5,000 × $2.10). The minimum price fluctuation (referred to as a "tick") in wheat is one-quarter cent, or $12.50 (5,000 × $0.0025), so a one-cent move in wheat is worth $50 per contract.

THE ROLES OF SPECULATORS AND HEDGERS IN FUTURES MARKETS

As mentioned previously, futures exchanges originated as vehicles for guarding against price fluctuations in agricultural commodities and for establishing a method of price discovery and trade for these items. The classic example is a farmer seeking to protect the value of his crop. In an uncertain market, the farmer has no idea what the prevailing price for the crop he is planting in the spring will be in the fall. If the bottom fell out of the market for some reason, he would have nothing to show for a season of work. To lock in a profit (or to buy insurance against a large price drop), a soybean farmer could sell November soybean futures, establishing the price at which he could sell his crop in the fall. If the price dropped, he is protected by his futures contract. If prices rise, he loses money on his futures contract but makes money on his physical crop. This process is called "hedging."

Speculators are those traders who are not hedging actual commodity or financial commodity holdings but are buying and selling to profit on price moves. They make up the other half of the futures market equation. Futures speculators range from commodity trading advisers (CTAs) trading billions of dollars in dozens of markets (much like stock portfolio managers) to pit traders and individuals, off-floor traders like you.

LEVERAGE AND MARGIN

Two of the most important concepts to understand in the futures markets are *margin* and *leverage*. Margin (the minimum amount of money you must have in your trading account to buy or to sell) in futures markets is much lower than it is the stock market. Leverage makes the large returns (and large losses) you hear so much about possible because it allows you to buy and to sell more futures contracts using much less capital than you would have to commit to the same dollar amount of stocks. The high percentage return this kind of leverage allows also creates a commensurate level of risk.

Margin in futures trading can be 5 percent or less, compared to the 50 percent minimum margin requirement for stocks. In spring 2000, a crude oil futures contract worth about $25,000 ($25 per barrel times a 1,000-barrel contract size) could be leveraged with margin of around $3,350, a little over 13 percent. Other markets have even lower margins in the 3 to 6 percent range. Minimum margin in the stock market is typically 50 percent.

Such low margins result from futures being contracts rather than actual assets. You are not exchanging anything in a futures trade; you are merely agreeing to do so at some point in the future. Additionally, margin for hedgers is lower than margin for speculators because a hedger's physical holdings (say, an oil refinery's reserves) function as collateral for the futures positions. Margin functions as a guarantee that you will be able to meet the financial obligations for your trades. Again, if your trade goes against you, you will be required to deposit more margin into your trading account.

Exchanges change the margin they assess their clearing firm members (i.e., your brokerage) based on the volatility of particular markets, among other factors. Your brokerage may then require more margin from you, even if the status of your position has not changed. There is no rule that says you have to use minimum margin, though. You could maintain 100 percent margin for all your futures positions, although the large size of most contracts can make this prohibitive.

Because of the low margin requirements in the futures markets, you can control large positions with relatively little money in your trading account. This is what makes returns in the futures markets potentially so large. What most traders conveniently ignore, though, is that their losses can be just as large. There is no such thing as a free lunch. This is why low-risk trading techniques are essential to success in the commodity markets.

Appendix II

OTHER POSSIBLY PROFITABLE METHODS

My purpose in this appendix is to point you toward things I have found to be profitable in my career. I will not be going into any detailed discussion of these methods, nor do I claim to have done any thorough investigation of any method related here. These are just things I have observed to work for others or have used for myself.

SPREAD TRADING

As I have described in this book, a thorough understanding of fundamentals is very useful, maybe even essential, for success in scale trading. Once you have done all that work to come up with a fundamental picture of a commodity, you are in a good position to spread trade. As described in Chapter 13, "The Dreaded Contract Rollovers," a *spread* is the buying of one thing and the selling of another. There are many kinds of spreads—intracommodity spreads, intercommodity spreads, crack spreads, crush spreads, and so on. I'm just referring to futures spreads. The number of different possible spreads using options is enormous.

The problem with spread trading is that each spread is unique. The most common type of spread is the intracommodity spread. In this type of spread the trader buys one month and sells another month in the same commodity. If he buys the near month and sells the back month, the spread is referred to as a bull spread; on the other hand, if he buys the back month and sells the near month, the spread is called a bear spread. The convention is to always put the month you are buying first when describing a spread. So the December/July corn spread is one in which you buy the December contract and sell the July.

The reason why a bear spread is one in which you buy the back month and a bull spread is one in which you buy the near month is that the near month is almost always more volatile than the back month. So, if the price goes up, the near month should go up more than the back month; and vice versa.

The reason I said each spread is unique is that there are so many fundamental factors involved in spreads. Some common spreads that spread traders use are the corn/wheat spread, the crack spreads between crude and its products (known as crack spreads because the process of refining crude oil is called "cracking"), and crush spreads between soybeans and its products (known as such because the process of making soybean meal and oil involves crushing a bean). In addition, traders spread cattle and hogs, hogs and pork bellies, and on and on.

Some common intracommodity spreads are the July/December corn spread, the July/November bean spread, and the April/June cattle spread. Each of these spreads is common because of unique tendencies that are based on fundamentals. For example, in the July/December corn spread, the July corn from last year's harvest will be delivered in July, and the December corn is this year's corn that is still growing. So it is an old crop/new crop spread. This spread is influenced very heavily by the change in crop size from year to year and by seasonal dynamics. The July/November bean spread is also an old crop/new crop spread.

Years ago I avoided spreads because they were too complicated. Because each spread had its own unique characteristics, it seemed to me that you had to learn those characteristics to trade spreads successfully, and that just seemed like too much to do. Over the years my involvement with scale trading has changed that opinion. Because I believe that successful scale trading hinges on good fundamental analysis, I have been deeply involved with fundamentals for years. This has enabled me to become familiar with the dynamics of a wide variety of commodity spreads.

Here are two factors I believe are necessary to be successful in trading commodity futures spreads:

1. Knowledge of the seasonal tendencies of those spreads.
2. Knowledge of the current fundamentals.

A trader with this knowledge can determine quickly whether he or she is interested in a particular spread. For information on the seasonal tendencies in spreads, I recommend Moore Research Center. You can find the firm on the Web at www.mrci.com. Armed with their information on the seasonal histories of various spreads and the fundamental knowledge you will have from your scale trading, you are in a good position. Seasonal tendencies have a fundamental cause. If you are well versed in the fundamentals of a particular commodity, you should be able to determine what the factors are that have driven the seasonal tendency of a particular spread. Once you can identify those fundamental factors, you can then check to see if those same fundamental factors exist this year. If they do, you are ready to take the last step I recommend before entering a spread: check the chart.

Most commercially available computer charting software packages can display spread charts. Here is a chart of the April/June crude oil spread (Figure A2.1), updated as of February 18, 2000. This is not a traditional seasonal chart, but I included it here to show how a bull spread behaves in a bull market. You can see the clear ongoing uptrend. Furthermore, you can see that trend lines can be applied to spread charts. In this case, I have drawn parallel lines known as channel lines.

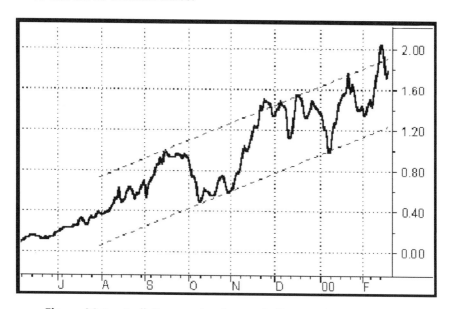

Figure A2.1 April–June crude oil spread. (*Source:* OmegaResearch)

Figure A2.2 shows the spread between June and August hogs on the same date, February 18, 2000. This shows a seasonal spread in the middle of its seasonal period, which Moore Research pegs as January 16 through March 13. This chart shows no clear trend. It actually clearly depicts a choppy market. A trader could choose to avoid this trade altogether but also could choose to wait to see if the spread moves either above this trading range (up around 500 points) or back to the bottom of the range (down around 260 points).

In the years that I have enjoyed using seasonal spreads, I have been happy with them because:

1. They give me another application for the fundamentals information I am gathering for scale trading.
2. I have been careful to check those fundamentals first before looking at a chart.
3. I have then checked the chart and applied very simple trend analysis, using trend lines to guide me on the precise entry and exit of these trades.

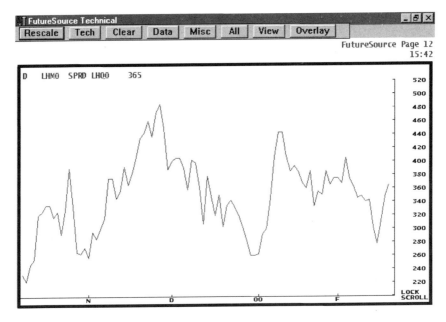

Figure A2.2 June–August hog futures spread. (*Source:* FutureSource/Bridge)

When I have deviated either from item 2 or item 3, I have been less pleased with the results.

DAY TRADING

If anything is the antithesis of scale trading, it would have to be day trading. Where scales are carefully considered long-term investments, day trades are intended to be quick in-and-out trades. In scale trading you want to carefully gather as much information as possible before deciding to enter into a scale. In day trading you need to be able to make quick decisions. Too much information tends to overwhelm the day trader, resulting in many missed trades while he or she takes time to consider all the data. Finally, scale trading is based on supply-and-demand fundamentals whereas day traders are almost always technical traders.

Although day trading is clearly the antithesis of scale trading, sometimes opposites can be complementary. I believe this can be one of those situations. The key here, and to what I have said about spread trading and about scale trading, is still doing your homework. The most successful traders I have known are also the hardest working. I do not in any way believe this to be a coincidence.

As with scale trading and spread trading, all the homework comes first. In the case of day trading, there are two kinds of homework. The first kind is the very difficult process of discovering what kind of methodology will suit your personality. I will describe what I am using currently, but I must tell you that I am always evolving my methods and seeking out new ideas from other traders. I recommend you do the same.

The second kind of homework is what I recommend that a trader do every day. Whether you do this in the afternoon to prepare for the next day or early in the morning before the trading day, I strongly recommend preparing for the trading day by finding out what reports are due out that day and by observing as many different things as you can about the character of the market. For example, is it oversold? Is it near support? Has it just broken out of a channel?

I prefer stock index futures for day trading. They have a long day, which gives me many opportunities. They have tremendous liquidity, which makes execution easier. And they have tremendous volatility. Without volatility it is very difficult to make money. I know other traders who day trade grains, bonds, metals, crude oil, and so on.

The main criteria for choosing a market should be *liquidity* and *volatility*. I would not like to day trade lumber, for example, because although it is volatile, the liquidity is so poor that I might actually lose money on good trades due to poor fills on my orders. Getting your orders executed cleanly can make the difference between profit and loss. Eurodollars are very liquid, but they often spend whole sessions trading just a few points. It is very hard to make money without price movement. Bonds are not very volatile, but they are much more volatile than Eurodollars and have a larger tick size. In the Eurodollars every tick is $25 so if it only moves four ticks today, you can only make a maximum of $100 per contract on any given trade. Bonds are $31.25 per tick and move a bit more. If bonds move only 10 ticks today, I have more profit potential than I have in Eurodollars.

There are many, many books on day trading, and I may write one of my own sometime. Right now I will just give the same kind of brief discussion as I did for spread trading.

One major difference between scale trading and day trading is that in day trading it is highly advisable to use stops. It is very likely that you will experience at least occasional losses, and it is very important that these be kept as small as possible. When you enter a trade, four things can result: (1) a large profit, (2) a large loss, (3) a small profit, and (4) a small loss. If you can eliminate the large losses, you can improve your probability of overall profit from your trading greatly. Trading without stops can make this difficult to do.

MY DAY TRADING METHOD

I did not invent this. I don't know who did. Most of it is common sense. To trade the way I do, you will need a computer and real-time quotes. You will also need a software package that will take your quote data and turn it into charts and indicators.

The first indicator I learned was stochastics. I doubt it is any better than any other indicator, such as %R, MACD, and Relative Strength Index. But, for me, stochastics is better because I have used it for years and have a better feel for it than the other ones.

Stochastics are made up of two elements, %K and %D. I have long ago forgotten which one is which, but one clearly moves faster than the other. Figure A2.3 shows stochastics for a 30-minute bar chart over several days in May 2000. Some traders who use stochastics pay attention to the crossover of the two lines for %K and %D. For my

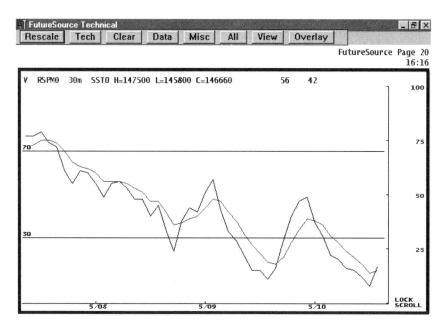

Figure A2.3   30-minute stochastics on S&P futures. (*Source:* FutureSource/ Bridge)

trading, I pay no attention to that at all. For my trading they may as well be one line.

Stochastics are drawn as an index from 0 to 100. Analysts interpret the movements in a variety of ways, including what constitutes overbought and oversold. However, for most analysts a reading of 30 percent or lower is oversold and 70 percent or higher is overbought, which is why I have drawn lines across the chart at those levels.

The first element of my method is to observe the stochastics across several different time frames. I start by looking at the stochastic on the daily chart. I then move to a 120-minute bar chart with stochastics and to 60-minute, 30-minute, 15-minute, and finally 5-minute stochastics. What I am looking for is alignment of the different time frames when they are in overbought or oversold mode.

Figure A2.4 shows the daily Standard & Poor's (S&P) chart with stochastics below it. On May 10, stochastics reached down to 10 percent. Looking at Figures A2.5 (120-minute), A2.6 (60-minute), A2.7 (30-minute), A2.8 (15-minute), and A2.9 (5-minute), you can see that

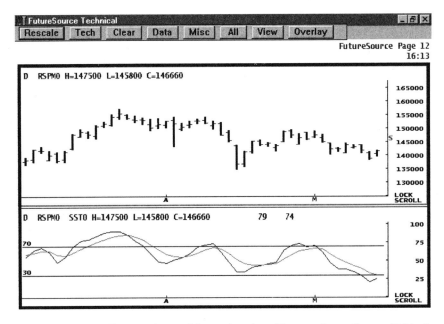

Figure A2.4 Daily S&P chart with stochastics. (*Source:* FutureSource/Bridge)

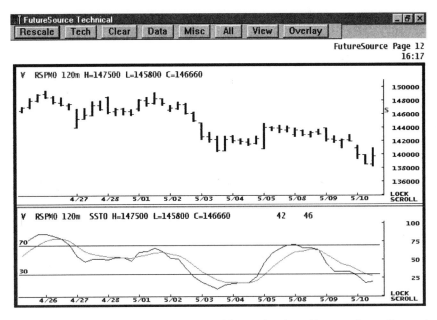

Figure A2.5 120-minute S&P chart with stochastics. (*Source:* FutureSource/ Bridge)

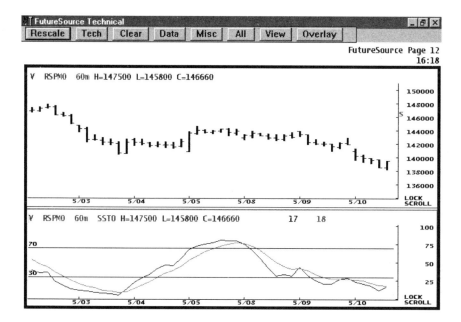

Figure A2.6 60-minute S&P chart with stochastics. (*Source:* FutureSource/ Bridge)

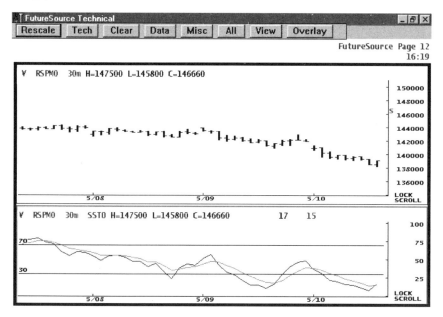

Figure A2.7 30-minute S&P chart with stochastics. (*Source:* FutureSource/ Bridge)

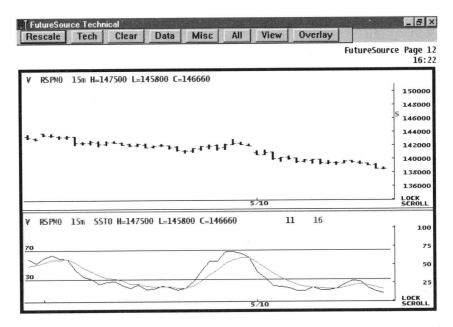

Figure A2.8 15-minute S&P chart with stochastics. (*Source:* FutureSource/ Bridge)

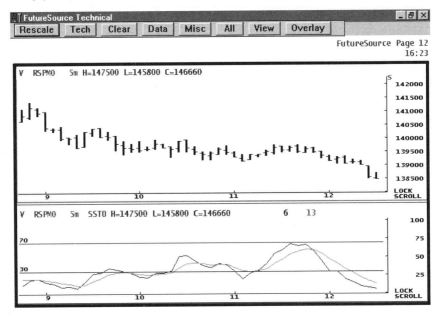

Figure A2.9 5-minute S&P chart with stochastics. (*Source:* FutureSource/ Bridge)

the March S&P was oversold in all time frames. So the first precondition for a trade is in place.

From here we are looking for some kind of rally. I could just buy at the market as soon as I have the precondition, but I don't recommend that. The problem is that in strong trending markets, I will get oversold or overbought readings for some time, and the trend will just continue. I recommend a simple trigger; there are many.

Now that the precondition has been achieved, I recommend getting rid of the stochastics and start following the price action. Many different methods can be used to trigger my entry, but because I am looking for a buy here. I want one that buys on strength. I don't want to buy a falling market until it has turned around. You may decide otherwise. One of our clients waits for situations like this and then scales in e-mini contracts in the S&P. That can work very well until you have a market that drops too far too fast. This is not scale trading, and it is a very big contract. Buying it without stops at nearly historical highs is too scary for me.

Figure A2.10 5-minute S&P chart with trend line. (*Source:* FutureSource/ Bridge)

Figure A2.10 shows how a simple trend line drawn on a 5-minute chart could have gotten you into this trade. Figure A2.11 shows what happened the rest of the day.

Depending on how you managed this trade, it could have been a great trade. Your entry would have been about 1388.60. The high of the move was 1403.50, almost 15 points above your entry point. A simple trailing stop might have taken you out at around 1398. Not bad.

And it takes me back to the introduction of this book. This kind of trade can get your greed juices going. It's exciting to think about how much money you could make this way. Well, it doesn't always work, so don't get too carried away. It's a good thing it works this well sometimes because you will need that money to overcome the losses you will have on the days when it doesn't work.

Use stops, be careful, do your homework, and good luck.

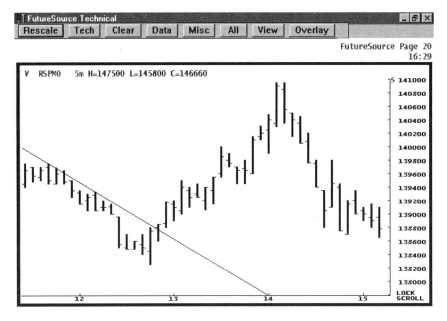

Figure A2.11 5-minute S&P chart showing trend line break and following results. (*Source:* FutureSource/Bridge)

CONCLUSION

There are methods other than scale trading that work. You only have to review the track records of money managers to know that. They don't all scale trade—far from it. Most are trend traders of one kind or another. Still, scale trading is a great method. I strongly recommend that it be the core of your futures investment strategy and that the couple of other methods to which I have alluded here only be adjuncts to your scale trading.

Spread trading does not require much margin, and day trading requires very little as well. That makes these two methods viable candidates for an account that is principally dedicated to scale trading but looking to diversify methodologies.

Appendix III

HOW TO CONSTRUCT A SCALE ON YOUR COMPUTER

This section is for use with Chapter 11 of this book. We have included in the back pocket of this book a 3¼-inch disk that provides a template of the scale spreadsheet in Microsoft Excel. The file is named scale.xls. Figure A3.1 is the spreadsheet that is on the disk.

Most spreadsheet programs ought to be able to open this file. We've also recorded it in several other formats on the disk.

PROCEDURE

1. In your spreadsheet program, copy the file named scale.xls to your computer. This will be your template.
2. Make a backup copy on your computer in case you accidentally mess up the template at some time.
3. Open the template. Give it the name of a scale you are going to try out. For example, if you are going to try soybeans in 2000, you could use the name bean00.xls.
4. Cells B1 through B8 are the "hot cells." That means that when you are using the spreadsheet to create each new scale, you change data *only* in those cells. All of the remaining formula cells look to these hot cells for their data. You control your scale solely through the hot cells. Here you change:
   - The commodity (noting the month).
   - The starting price of your scale.

RECOMMENDED SCALE TRADE PLAN

Commodity:

Month:

Starting price:

Maintenance margin:

Profit/loss per $:

Buy-down increment:

Sell-profit increment:

Total buy levels:

Contracts at each level:

	1				2	3	4	5	6	7	8
Buy Level	Buy Price	Date Order Placed	Date Order Filled	Sell Price	Date Order Placed	Date Order Filled	No. of Contracts Held	Losing Contracts	Loss per Contract	Possible Cumulative Loss per Contract	Possible Cumulative Loss on All Contracts	Cumulative Required Margin	Minimum Account Funds
1													
2													
3													
4													
5													
6													
7													
8													

Figure A3.1   Master Scale Trade Worksheet.

- The margin from the *current* margin sheet provided by the clearing house through which you are trading (not just any clearing house, as they may be slightly different).
- The profit or loss per contract that you expect—the increments of your buy-downs.
- The number of contracts you expect to buy.
- The number of contracts per level.

We have made the hot cell numbers boldface and colored. This will remind you not to ruin your spreadsheet by accidentally typing in a formula cell.

5. You never touch the other "formula" cells. The computer takes the "hot cell" numbers and plugs them into the formula cells automatically.

6. Be sure to make a backup of the template and to rename the template as your new scale each time—*before* you begin work.

GLOSSARY

Actuals   Products bought and sold in the spot market. Also known as *physicals.*

Arbitrage   Simultaneous purchase or sale of a contract in different markets to profit from discrepancies in prices between those markets.

Assignment   Notice to an option writer that an option has been exercised by the option holder.

At-the-Money Option   An option whose exercise price is equal or nearly equal to the current market price of the underlying futures contract.

Backwardation   Market condition in which the price of the front month is higher than prices of the back months. Also known as *inverted market.*

Basis   Difference between the spot price and the price of the futures.

Bear   A person who believes prices will decline; opposite of *bull.*

Bear Market   A market in which prices are declining.

Bid   Offer to purchase at a specified price.

Break   Sharp rapid decline in price.

Broker   Firm or person who handles the execution of another party's trades.

Bull   A person who believes prices will rise; opposite of *bear.*

Bull Market   A market in which prices are rising.

Buyer   The purchaser of an option, either a call option or a put option. Also referred to as *option holder*. An option purchase may be in connection with either an opening or a closing transaction.

Call Option   An option that gives the holder the right *to buy* (go "long") the underlying futures contract, commodity, or security at a fixed price any time prior to the expiration of the option contract.

Car   An old term sometimes used to describe a contract ("car of bellies," for example); coming from a time when quantities of the product specified on a contract often corresponded closely to the quantity carried in a railroad car.

Carrying Charges   Cost of storing a physical commodity over a period of time; includes insurance and interest on the invested funds, as well as other incidental costs.

Clearing Corporation   The corporation whose function it is to clear (match) all purchases and sales and to ensure the financial integrity of all futures and options transactions on the exchange where traded. Once a trade has been cleared, the Clearing Corporation becomes the buyer to every seller and the seller to every buyer.

Clearing Member   A member of the clearinghouse or association. All trades of a nonclearing member must be registered and eventually settled through a clearing member.

Clerk   A member's employee who works on the trading floor as a phone person or runner.

Closing Transacton   A closing transaction is one which closes out a position; offets an open position in one's account. In the case of a short position the closing transaction would be a buy.

Commission   Fee charged by a broker to a customer when a transaction is made.

Commodity   A raw material, normally traded using a standard grade, for example, #2 heating oil. Commodity contracts come in standardized sizes.

Commodity Futures Trading Commission (CFTC)   The regulatory agency of the U.S. government that supervises the trading activities of commodity and domestic commodity option exchanges.

Commodity Pool The combined funds of several people; used for trading futures or options for profits.

Commodity Trading Adviser (CTA) A person who advises others about buying or selling futures contracts or options or who trades on the customer's behalf. A CTA trades other people's money; must be registered with the CFTC.

Contango Market condition when the price of the front month is lower than prices of the back months. This is normal for most markets because back months include carrying charges (interest, storage, etc.).

Contract A unit of trading in futures or options, similar to *round lot* in securities markets; also, actual bilateral agreement between buyer and seller in a futures transaction.

Contract Month Month in which futures contracts may be satisfied by making or accepting delivery. Also known as *delivery month*.

Covered Option An option that is written against an opposite position in the underlying futures contract or commodity at the time of execution or placement of the order.

Covered Writer The seller of a covered option.

Customer Account Account established by the clearing member solely for the purpose of clearing exchange transactions by the clearing member on behalf of its customers other than those transactions of a floor trader.

Day Trading Establishing and liquidating the same position or positions within the same trading session.

Deferred Futures Futures contracts that expire during the more distant months.

Delivery The tender and receipt of an actual commodity, warehouse receipt, or other negotiable instrument covering such commodity in settlement of a futures contract.

Domestic Commodity Market A U.S. board of trade licensed by the CFTC to list a commodity option for trading. Also known as *option exchange market, contract market*.

Exchange The marketplace where commodity futures contracts and options on them are traded. U.S. exchanges are regulated by the Commodity Exchange Act.

Exercise The action taken by the holder of a call if he or she wishes to purchase the underlying futures contract or by the holder of a put if he or she wishes to sell the underlying futures contract.

Exercise Price Price specified in the option contract at which the underlying futures contract or commodity position is established on exercise of the option contract.

Expiration The date after which a futures contract can no longer trade or an option may no longer be exercised. (Although options expire on a specified date the preceding month, an option on a December futures contract is referred to as a "December option" because exercise would lead to the creation of a December futures position.)

First Notice Day The first date, varying by commodities and exchanges, on which notices of intentions to deliver actual commodities against futures are authorized.

Floor Broker A member who executes orders for the account of one or more clearing members.

Floor Trader A member who executes trades for his or her own account or for an account controlled by him or her. Also referred to as *local*.

Futures Commission Merchant (FCM) A firm or person engaged in soliciting or accepting and handling orders for the purchase or sale of commodities for future delivery on, or subject to, the rules of a futures exchange and who, in connection with such solicitation or acceptance of orders, accepts any money or securities to margin any resulting trades or contracts; must be licensed under the Commodity Exchange Act.

Futures Contract A contract traded on a futures exchange for the delivery of a specified commodity or financial instrument at a future time. The contract specifies the item to be delivered and the terms and conditions of delivery.

Futures Price The price of a particular futures contract determined by open competition between buyers and sellers on the trading floor or the exchange.

Hedge The buying or selling of offsetting positions to provide protection against an adverse change in price. A hedge may involve having positions in the cash market, the futures market, and/or options.

House Account An account established by the clearing member solely for the purpose of clearing exchange transactions by the clearing member on behalf of persons who qualify under Regulation 1.3(Y) (I-VIII) issued by the CFTC.

In-the-Money Option A call whose exercise price is below the current price of the underlying futures contract (i.e., if the option has intrinsic value); a put whose exercise price is above the current price of the underlying futures contract.

Intrinsic Value The dollar amount that could be realized if the option were to be currently exercised. *See* In-the-Money option.

Introducing Broker A CTFC/NFA registered broker who solicits and services customer brokerage accounts but "introduces" (passes on) their orders to Futures Commission Merchants for execution, clearing, and record keeping.

Inverted Market A futures market in which the nearer months are selling at premiums to the more distant months. Also known as *backwardation*.

Last Trading Day Final day under an exchange's rules during which trading may take place in a particular futures delivery month. Futures contracts outstanding at the end of the last trading day must be settled by delivery or, in the case of cash settlement, by an exchange of cash value differences.

Liquidation Any transaction that closes out a long or short position. Also known as *offset*.

Liquidity The condition of a market such that it has a high level of trading activity, allowing buying and selling with minimum price disturbance.

Local A floor broker who usually executes trades only for his own account.

Long The position established by the purchase of a futures contract or an option (either a call or a put) if there is no offsetting position.

Margin The sum of money that must be deposited with and maintained by account owner to provide protection to both parties in a trade. The exchange establishes minimum margin amounts that customers must deposit with their brokerage firms. In turn, brokerage firms must post and maintain margin with the Clearing Corporation. Buyers of options do not have to post margin because their risk is limited to the option premium.

Margin Calls   Additional funds that a person with a futures position or the writer of an option may be required to deposit if there is an adverse price change or if margin requirements are increased. Buyers of options are not subject to margin calls.

Naked Writing   Writing a call or a put on a futures contract in which the writer has no opposite cash or futures market position. Also known as *uncovered writing.*

National Futures Association (NFA)   Self regulatory industry association. They operate under the auspices of the CFTC to enforce the rules of the Commodity Exchange Act of the CFTC.

Offset   *See* Liquidation.

Open Interest   Number of open contracts. Refers to unliquidated purchases or sales, never to their combined total.

Open, The   The varying time period at the beginning of the trading session officially designated by the exchange during which all transactions are considered made "at the opening." The precise time varies with the amount of activity at the opening.

Opening Price   The price (or range) recorded during the period designated by the exchange at the official opening.

Opening Transaction   A purchase or sale that establishes a new position.

Option   A contract with a seller and a buyer that gives the buyer the right, but not the obligation, to buy or to sell the underlying instrument.

Option Class   All option contracts of the same type covering the same underlying futures contract, commodity, or security.

Option Grantor   A person who, in exchange for the premium, has agreed to assume the opposite side of an exercise at a fixed price any time prior to the expiration of the contract in the underlying futures contract, commodity, or security, should he or she be called on to do so.

Option Type   The classification of an option contract as either a put or a call.

Orders—Cancel-Replace An order that instructs the floor broker to cancel a previous order immediately and to enter a new order to replace the previous order.

Orders—Day Orders An order not specified as GTC or open or as good until a specific date and time. A day order is automatically canceled at the end of the trading session if it is not filled or canceled before that time.

Orders—Fill or Kill Order A quick order to fill or to kill is a limit order placed close to the prevailing market price to be executed immediately upon receipt at the specified limit or kill (cancel) the order.

Orders—Good 'til Canceled, (GTC) Order An open order that remains in force until it is canceled or filled or until the contract to which it applies expires.

Orders—Limit Order An order to be executed at the stated price or better; can be to buy or to sell.

Orders—Market if Touched A straight limit order with the additional understanding that, if the market reaches the limit without the broker being able to fill all or part, the order is to become a *market order.*

Orders—Market on Close A day order that is to be executed at the market during the closing range only.

Orders—Market on Opening A day order that is to be executed at the market during the opening range only.

Orders—Market Order An order placed to be executed at the best possible price at the time the order reaches the floor broker.

Orders—One Cancels Other Order An order that instructs the floor broker that the order may be filled at one of the two limits indicated; once the order is filled at one limit, the second indicated limit is immediately canceled.

Orders—"Or Better" Limit Order A qualifying order that is to be used only when the selling limit is below or when the buying limit is above the prevailing market price.

Orders—Stop Limit Order An order that specifies that when the market reaches the specified stop price, the order becomes a *limit order* and not a market order.

Orders—Stop Order   An order that specifies a price at which the resting stop order becomes a *market order* and is executed at the best possible price.

Orders—Straddle Order   The simultaneous purchase and sale of one commodity of different contract months.

Orders—Straight Cancellation Order   Instruction order to cancel a previous order immediately with no further instructions.

Out-of-the-Money Option   A put or call option that currently has no intrinsic value; a call whose exercise price is above the current futures price or a put whose exercise price is below the current futures price.

Overbought   A market that has had a sharp decline. Rank-and-file traders (who were bullish and long earlier) have turned bearish.

Oversold   A market that has had a sharp upturn. Rank-and-file traders (who were bearish and short earlier) have turned bullish.

Point   Unit used for calculating the value of futures or options.

Premium   The price of an option contract, without any charges or fees, paid by the purchaser to the seller for the right to purchase (call) or sell (put) the underlying futures contract, commodity, or security at a fixed price any time prior to the expiration of the contract.

Proprietary Account   Account established by the clearing member solely for the purpose of clearing exchange transactions by the clearing member on behalf of itself.

Put Option   An option that gives the option buyer the right *to sell* (go "short") the underlying futures contact at the exercise price on or before the expiration date.

Resistance   A price point at which prices hit an invisible barrier. *See* Support.

Round Turn   The purchase and sale of a contract. The long or short position of an individual is offset by an opposite transaction or by accepting or making delivery of the actual commodity.

Scale Trading   A method for buying into a declining market, then setting profit targets for each individual contract bought.

Scalp   Trading for small gains. Involves establishing and liquidating a position quickly, within the same day, hour, or minute.

Security Deposit   Funds that must be deposited by a customer with his or her broker for each futures contract as a guarantee of fulfillment of the contract. It is not considered part payment of purchase. Used interchangeably with *margin*.

Security Deposit Call   A demand for additional cash funds because of adverse price movement. Better known as *margin call*.

Settlement Price   Daily price at which the clearinghouse clears all trades and settles all accounts between clearing members for each contract month. Settlement prices are used to determine both margin calls and invoice prices for deliveries.

Short   The position created by the sale of a futures contract or option (either a call or a put) if there is no offsetting position.

Spread   A position consisting of both long and short options of the same class, such as having a long position in a call with one exercise price and expiration and a short position in another call with a different exercise price and/or expiration.

Straddle   A combination in which the put and the call have the same exercise price and the same expiration.

Strike Price   The price specified in the option contact on which the underlying futures contract, commodity, or security is established at exercise of the option contract.

Support   A price point at which prices find an invisible base. *See* Resistance.

Tick   Refers to minimum change in price. Also known as *point* or *basis point*.

Time Value   Any amount by which an option premium exceeds the option's intrinsic value. If an option has no intrinsic value, its premium is entirely time value.

Trend   General direction of market prices.

Uncovered Option   An option that is written without having an opposite position in the underlying futures contract, commodity, or security.

Underlying Futures Contract   The specific futures contract that can be bought or sold by the exercise of an option.

Volume   The number of purchases or sales of a commodity futures contract made during a specified period of time.

Writing   The sale of an option in an option transaction.

INDEX

Adjustments, scale, 125–126
Advertising, 150–151
Agribusiness, 59
American Eagles, 73–74
American Petroleum Institute, 82
At-the-money options, 141–142

Back months, 162
Backward market, 127
Bankruptcy, 61, 146
Baruch, Bernard, 115
Bean crops, 53–54
Bearish market, 26, 66
Bear market, 120
Bear spread, 167–168
Beef consumption, 62
Blue chip stocks, 15
Boom-bust cycle, 12
Bottom-picking, 114
BP Amoco, 83
Brazil, bean crops in, 53–54
Breakout traders, 28
Breeding stock, 61
Bretton Woods accord, 70

Brokers:
  full-service, 20–21, 125, 158
  relationship with, 152, 156
  selection factors. *See* Broker selection factors
  services provided, 149–153
Broker selection factors:
  brokerage services, 149–153
  commissions, 153–157
  FCM service, 147–148
  importance of, 130
  interest *vs.* T-bills, 157–158
  margins, 158–159
  regulatory history, 148–149
  security, 145–147
Building a position, 8
Bullish market, 26
Bull market, 120
Bull spread, 167
Business Week, 70
Buy low, sell high strategy, 7–8
Buy the rumor, sell the fact strategy, 42

Calendar spread, 124
Calf-breeding operations, 61
Call options, 136, 138–143
Canola oil, 52
Capital requirements, 17, 34,
    111–112
Carryin, 46
Carrying charges, 45, 127–129
Carryout, 47
Cash price, 128
Cash settlement, 163–164
Cattle, 59–63
Cattle-on-Feed report, 59–60
Central banks, 73
Channel lines, 169
Charts:
    day trading and, 169
    seasonal, 93–95
    significance of, 26–27, 34
Chicago Board of Trade (CBOT),
    15, 54–55, 70, 112, 162
Chicago Mercantile Exchange
    (CME), 70–71, 91, 112, 146
Chicago wheat, 55
Christian Precious Metals, 73
Clearinghouse, 156
Cocoa, 85–86, 130
Coffee, 87–88
Cold storage report, 67–68
Comex Warehouse Stocks, 75
Commissions:
    appropriate amounts, 157
    brokers, types of, 152–154
    discount brokers, 154, 158
    full-service brokers, 114,
        129
    online brokers, 154–156
Commodity:
    defined, 16–18
    value of, 16

Commodity Exchange Act,
    146
Commodity Futures Trading
    Commission (CFTC),
    148
*Commodity Traders Consumer
    Report* (CTCR), 32–33
Commodity trading, overview,
    3–4
Commodity trading advisers
    (CTAs), 164–165
Company reports, as information
    resource, 150
*Complete Guide to the Futures
    Markets: Fundamental and
    Technical Analysis*
    (Schwager), 47
Constructing a scale. *See* Scale
    construction
Contingency orders, 155–156
Contract months, 162
Contract sizes, 135, 164
Contrarian trading, 115
Copper:
    demand, 76–77
    supplies, 75–76
Corn, 54, 164
Cotton, 89
Covered call, 141
CPM Group, 79
Cracking, 168
Crop reports, monthly,
    50–51
Crown Futures Corporation,
    150–151, 153
Crude oil, 81–83, 89
Cultural changes, impact of,
    75
Currencies, 70–72
Currency futures, 16, 163

Cutbacks, evidence of, 43–44, 45, 66
Cyclical commodities, 17
Cyclical market, hogs, 65

Day trading, 171–178
Delivery, cash settlement *vs.*, 163–164
Delivery months, 162
Delta, 141–142
Demonetization:
  of gold, 70–72
  of silver, 73–74
Discount brokers, 154, 158
Dow Jones Industrial Average, 15
Drawdowns, 34, 122, 131–134, 158

Economic conditions, livestock futures and, 62
Elasticity, supply and demand, 11–12
Ending stocks, 46
Energy market:
  crude oil, 81–82, 89
  defined, 163
  energy statistics, 82–83
  unleaded gasoline, 82
Entry strategies, 170
Eurodollars, 172
Exchanges:
  FCM membership, 146–147
  margin and, 165
Executions:
  drawdowns and, 132, 134
  rollovers, 127
  put options, 137–138
Exercise price, 134
Exit strategies, 113, 170
Extrinsic value, 136

Falling market, 32, 136, 177
False breakouts, 28
False signals, 32
FCM (Futures Commission Merchant) service, 145–148, 158
Fear, dealing with, 113
Federal Deposit Insurance Corporation (FDIC), 145
Feeder cattle, 63–64
Feedlots, cattle, 60–62
Financial futures, 17–18, 163
First Notice Day, 123–125, 129–130, 163
F.O. Licht Company, 86
Foreign Agricultural Service, USDA, 88
Friedman, Milton, 70–71
Front month, 162
Full-service brokers:
  commissions, 153, 158
  discount brokers compared with, 154, 158
  functions of, 20–21, 125, 158
Fundamental analysis:
  components of, 19–21
  do-it-yourself guide, 46–47
Fundamental Analysis (Schwager), 47
Fundamental analyst, selection of, 41
Fundamentals:
  currencies, 163
  cutback, evidence of, 43–44, 45
  defined, 41–43
  energy market, 81–83, 163
  financials, 163
  grain market, 49–57, 163
  livestock market, 59–68, 163
  metals market, 69–79, 163

Fundamentals *(Continued)*
  price range, 43
  seasonal information and,
    91–95
  softs market, 85–89, 163
Futures contracts:
  characteristics of, 161–163
  historical perspective, 71
Futures price, 128

Gambling system, 4, 6
Gold:
  balance sheet, 72–73
  demonetization of, 70–72
  overview, 69–70
  supplies, 72
Gold and Silver Institute, 75
Good-til-canceled (GTC) orders,
    152–153
Grain market fundamentals:
  corn, 54
  overview, 49–51, 163
  prices, stocks-to-use ratios,
    56–57
  soybean complex, 51–54
  wheat, 54–56
Grain Stocks report, 51
Grandmill, William, 56
Great Depression, 65
Greed, 178
Green cattle, 61
Gross Domestic Product (GDP),
    76–77
Groundnut oil, 52

Hard commodities, 18
Head-and-shoulders tops, 8
Heating oil, 82–83, 92–93
Hedgers, 164–165
Historical prices, 21–22

Hogs and Pigs report, 64–67, 68
Hold-back programs, 87

Interest rates, impact of, 16, 42,
    127
International Cocoa
    Organization (ICCO), 86
International Coffee
    Organization (ICO), 87
International Copper Study
    Group, 77
International Monetary Fund,
    73
Internet service provider (ISP),
    156
Intervals, buying, 110–111
In-the-money option, 136–137
Intracommodity spread, 167
Intrinsic value, 17–18, 136, 142
Inventory, buying, 114–115
*Investing in Wheat, Corn, and
    Soybeans* (Grandmill),
    56–57
Investor's Business Daily, 42

Japanese yen, 16, 163
Johnson Mathey, 79

Kansas City Board of Trade
    (KCBOT), 55
Kansas City wheat, 55
Kept-for-breeding hogs, 66
Keynes, John Maynard, 70

Leverage, 165
Limit order, 124
Liquidation, of cattle supply, 61
Liquidity:
  day trading and, 172
  of rollovers, 128–129

Livestock market:
  cattle, 59–63
  defined, 59, 163
  feeder cattle, 63–64
  hogs, 64–67
  pork bellies, 67–68
Locals, 30
Long positions, 112, 132, 162
Long scales, 18–19
Long-term systematic commodity
    fund managers, 4
Losing positions, 31
Loss, transparent, 126–127

Margin, 105, 114, 158–159,
    165–166
Margin call, 157
Market bottoms, 18–19
Market conditions, 34
Market indicators, 120
Marketings, Cattle-on-Feed
    reports, 60
Market order, 124, 147
Market-ready animals, 61
Market tops, 18–19
Megatraders, 7
Metals market:
  copper, 75–77
  defined, 163
  gold, 69–73
  platinum, 77–79
  silver, 73–75
Microsoft Excel spreadsheets,
    109, 181
MidAmerica Commodity
    Exchange (MidAm),
    111–112
Mine production:
  copper, 75–76
  gold, 73

platinum, 77, 106–107
silver, 74
Minneapolis Grain Exchange
    (MGE), 55
Minneapolis wheat, 55
Moore, Steve, 91, 93
Moore Research Center, 91, 93,
    169–170
Moving average, 35, 120, 172
Multiple contracts, 162–163

Naked short options, 141
Narrow-range trading, 112
National Futures Association
    (NFA), 148–149
National Oil Processors
    Association (NOPA), as
    information resource, 53
Net disinvestment, 73
Net producer hedging, 73
Neutral market, 26
Newsletters, as information
    resource, 41, 150
News stories, impact of,
    42–43
New York Board of Trade,
    Coffee, Sugar, and Cocoa
    Division, 87
New York Cotton Exchange, 18
Nixon, Richard, 70, 73

Official sector sales, 73
1–2-3 bottoms, 8
Online brokers, 154–156
Optimization, 35, 37
Options:
  call, 138–143
  defined, 134
  drawdowns, 131–134
  put, 137–138

Options *(Continued)*
types of, 134–135
value of, 135–137
Organization of Petroleum
Exporting Countries
(OPEC), 81
Oscillation:
profits, 129
put options and, 138
trades, 112, 155
Out-of-the-money option,
136–137, 142
Overpriced market, 43

Palm oil, 52–53
Paper losses, 114
Patience, importance of, 22–24
%D, 172
%K, 172
%R, 35, 172
Placements, Cattle-on-Feed
report, 60
Planting Intentions report, 50–51
Platinum:
balance sheet, 79
demand, 78–79, 107
scale construction, 105–109
supplies, 77–78, 107
Pork bellies, 67–68, 164
Premium, call/put, 136, 138,
142
Price charts, benefits of, 21
Price range, 43
Profit objectives, 126
Profit-taking:
generally, 42
planning profits, 120–122
planning sells, 117–120
Purchases, in allotments, 6. *See
also* Contract sizes
Put options, 56, 136–138

Rallies, 8, 31–32, 177
Rapeseed oil, 52
Recession, 62, 82
Relative strength, 35, 172
Risk/reward analysis, 34–35, 49,
142–143
Rollovers:
avoidance strategies,
129–130
carrying charges, 127–128
defined, 123, 163
execution of, 127
fine-tuning guidelines,
124–125
First Notice Day, 123–125,
129–130, 163
to liquidity, 128–129
profit objectives, 126
scale adjustment, 125–126
seasonal tendencies, 127, 129,
168
transparent loss, 126–127
to volatility, 128–129

Scale construction:
buying intervals, 110–111
computer programs for,
109–110, 181–183
inventory, buying, 114–115
modifications, 111–112
oscillation trades, 112
platinum scale, 105–109
soybean oil scale, 99–105
stops, 113–114
Scale-down basis, 15–16
Scale trading:
advantages to, 7–9
characteristics of, generally, 3,
7
other types of trading
compared with, 25–38

purchases, 6
timing of, 11–24
ScaleTrading.com, 159
Schwager, Jack, 47
Seasonal information:
  rollovers and, 127, 129
  seasonal charts, 93–95
  seasonal tendencies, 24,
    91–93, 127, 129,
    168–169
Seasonal Pattern Charts, 93
Seasonal spreads, 170
Seasonal tendencies, 24, 91–93,
  127, 129, 164–169
Securities Investor Protection
  Corporation (SIPC), 145
Security, as broker selection
  factor, 145–147
Sells, planning strategy,
  117–120
Short sales, 28, 138–139, 141
Short-term pit traders, 4
Sideways market, 27–28, 120
Silver:
  balance sheet, 75
  culture changes, impact on,
    75
  demonetization of, 73–74
  supplies, 74–75
Silver certificates, 73
Simple moving average, 35
Slippage, 147
Softs market fundamentals:
  cocoa, 85–86
  coffee, 87–88
  cotton, 89
  defined, 163
  sugar, 88
Software programs:
  charting, 169
  technical analysis, 19

Soybean complex:
  bean crops, Brazil, 53–54
  soybean meal and oil, 52–53
  soybeans, 51–52
Soybean meal, 52–53, 164
Soybean oil:
  contract size, 164
  fundamentals, 52–53
  scale construction, 99–105
Soybeans, 51–52
Speculation, 56
Speculators, 164–165
Spikes, implications of, 22, 61
Spread, defined, 124, 167
Spread chart, 125
Spread orders, rollovers and, 124
Spreadsheets, 109, 181
Spread trading, 53, 167–171, 179
Standard & Poor's 500 Index,
  16–17, 135
Step II export subsidy program,
  89
Stochastics, 35, 172–177
Stocks-to-use ratio:
  defined, 46–47
  gold market, 73
  grain market, 50, 56–57
  sugar, 88
Stops:
  implications of, 30–34, 147
  scale construction and,
    113–114
Strike price, 134, 136, 141
Sugar, 88
Sunflower oil, 52
Supply and demand. *See also*
  Fundamentals; Seasonal
  information
  gold market, 72–73
  implications of, 11–19, 21, 38.
Swiss franc, 163

Technical analysis, 19–20, 26
Technological advances, impact of, 71, 92, 109–110
Third world countries, 83, 85
Tick, defined, 164
Time decay, 137–138
Trading primer:
  commodity groups, 163
  contract sizes, 164
  delivery, cash settlement vs., 163–164
  futures contracts, 161–163
  hedgers, 164
  leverage, 165
  margin, 165–166
  speculators, 164–165
Trading range, bottom third of, 21–22
Trading systems, types of, 35, 37. See also Day trading; Spread trading
Trailing stop, 30
Transparent loss, 126–127
Treasury bills (T-bills), 157–158
Trend-following systems, 26–29
Trend lines, 170, 177
Trends, implications of, 8
Trend stability, sensitivity vs. 34–38
Trend trading, pitfalls of, 32

Underpriced market, 43
U.S. Census Bureau, 53
United States Department of Agriculture (USDA), as information resource, 49–51, 56, 59–60, 65–66, 87–89

U.S. Department of Defense, 73
U.S. Department of Energy, as information resource, 82–83
U.S. dollar, 70–71, 163
U.S. Dollar Index, 16
U.S. Treasury bond futures, 16
Unleaded gasoline, 4–5, 82

Value. See Extrinsic value; Intrinsic value
Volatility:
  day trading and, 172
  emotion and, 18–19
  hog market and, 68
  options and, 136
  planning profits and, 120–122
  rollovers and, 128–129
  scale construction, 111

Wall Street Journal, 42
Wasting asset, 137
Wheat:
  contract sizes, 164
  global, 55–56
  kinds of, 55
  news stories, 56
  seasonal chart for, 93–94
World Bank, 73
World Gold Council, 73
World market, 70, 86

For more information about the disk, please see Appendix III on pages 181–183.